The Enigma of Love

Human and Divine

DAVID THEODORE CLAYTON

THE CHOIR PRESS

Republished in the United Kingdom in 2017 by
The Choir Press

ISBN 978-1-911589-17-4

Dedication

I dedicate this book to all those who have helped and encouraged me in my spiritual journey, and who still do.

I wish to thank my publishers for their help and advice during the publication process and a special word of thanks for Helen Orr who translated my hand written work into readable computerised script, to my wife Marion for her patience and proof reading of the text. I also thank Professor Keith Ward Regius Professor of Divinity Emeritus at the University of Oxford for kindly agreeing to read an early draft of my work, and encouraging me to continue with the project. I express my appreciation to Mrs Judy Powles Librarian at Spurgeon's College for the use of the library facilities and my thanks to those copyright holders who have given me permission to quote from various works.

To any Copyright Holders that I have not contacted, not been able to contact, unable to trace, the author and publisher would be pleased to be contacted so that in any future editions of this book acknowledgement can be made.

Table of Contents

"If you want to be a friend of all people, generate love and compassion.If you want to be a spiritual guide for all people, generate love and compassion. If you want to help everyone, generate love and compassion." Even if you searched for eons to find the best method to achieve permanent happiness, you would find that the only way is to generate love and compassion.

(The Tibeten lama Kunu Tenzin Gyelsten)

Quoted in, Widening The Circle of Love, His Holiness the Dalai Lama.

Introduction

For all, the meaning that one soul can pour into their life in this earthly span limited as it is to some few decades, does it all end in dust and ashes. Is there a truth which is actually evidenced in the present but which it is impossible to contain within any one life? Is there an exciting fulfilling enhancing principle which because of its very quality, its very essence, is of endurable and everlasting content? A quality that actually brings such meaning and purpose to life that it gives hope for the present which transcends a pessimist's limited vision, and discovers a reality that includes the present but goes beyond it? Discovers a reality which we can glimpse here, discovering more of its depths as time moves on until in the theology of hope it inevitably shines with cosmic light beyond the confines of present human comprehension; which we can tentatively touch, see in the 'now', even as it were squinting through a fog, the shape of that which makes life bigger than we can possibly imagine? I would maintain that there is, and when explored and activated brings meaning, purpose and life, now and forever.

Tolstoy wrote, "I believe that true human salvation consists in the fulfilment of the will of God, but that his will is for human beings to love one another, and therefore to act towards one another as they would want others to act towards them; as it says in the Gospel, that this is the whole meaning of the law and the prophets ...

I believe that the meaning of the life of each individual consists merely in the intensification of love itself, that these intensifications of love lead the individual to ever greater salvation in this life, and that life brings all the greater salvation, the more love there is in a person, and at the same time contributes most to the bringing about of the kingdom of God in the world, i.e. an order of life under which the now prevalent division, treachery and violence will be replaced among human beings by the former harmony, truth and brotherly love."[1]

Martin Buber, the great Jewish religious philosopher, wrote ... "Existence will remain meaningless for you if you yourself do not penetrate into it with active love, and if you do not in this way discover its meaning for yourself. Everything is waiting to be hallowed by you; it is waiting for this meaning to be disclosed and realised by you ... meet the world with the fullness of your being and you shall meet God. If you wish to believe, love!"[2]

William Barclay, the well known 20th century New Testament scholar, wrote that the love we see in the New Testament which the early Christians named agape ... "is that unconquerable benevolence, that undefeatable good-

---

1   Quoted in 'The Poet as a Mirror' Karl Josef Kuschel SCM (ID) p.318

2   Quoted in Visions of Love, William Sykes, Bible Reading Fellowship 1992 p.152

will, which will never seek anything but the highest good of others, no matter what they do to us, and no matter how they treat us." "Christian thought fastened on this word agape, because it was the only word capable of being filled with the content which was required. The great reason why Christian thought fastened on agape is that agape demands the exercise of the whole man. Christian love must not only extend to our nearest and dearest, our kith and kin, our friends and those who love us; Christian love must extend to the Christian fellowship, to the neighbour, to the enemy, to the entire world."[3]

This is the enigma of love, agape – it is different from every other form of love.

This I maintain is the principle for living; this brings meaning to life temporal and eternal. It is this which infuses hope and faith, which will see the hopeless and faithless through to ultimate salvation for this life and beyond. This is the enigma of love which we will explore, seeing it as the answer to life's' questions. We see this in aspects of love which in real situations has been the answer for a host of different people; giving hope to the hopeless, and life to the lifeless. The whole emphasis in this work will be in seeing what I describe as the silver lining in life, whether we are dealing with the dark places in human history, or in looking at the ultimate meaning and purpose of the universe in cosmic and personal terms. This is not to say we should turn a blind eye to problems. There are a host of books that face head-on the problems in our world,

---

3   William Barclay, Commentary of Matthew's Gospel, St Andrews Press, revised edition 1975 p.224, and 'New Testament Words' SCM 1964 p.20

seeking and suggesting solutions, and we are most grateful for all the positive and helpful work that has been, and is being, done.

I write from within a Christian tradition, but this love is expressed across all cultures, religions, backgrounds, believers and unbelievers.

My emphasis is on the good in our world which is as much a fact as the evil. One fact does not cancel out another here. It is a fact in every decade of recorded history that good takes place, that the incredible enigma 'love', the love Jesus advocated against all odds, is victorious again and again, an enigma that will bring in ultimate salvation.

Philip Yancey writes in the 1990's, "People shake their heads in despair over the state of the world despite the fact that in the last decade six hundred million people gained freedom from the greatest tyranny of our century, with hardly a shot being fired. In Eastern Europe a god fell to earth like an idol knocked from its pedestal by a bolt of lightning, and at its base stood Christians armed with nothing but the power of prayer. In South Africa, the leader of the last theologically, racist party on earth led the way toward reconciliation. Why the change? F.W. De Klerk himself gave the reason: After his inauguration, in tears, he told his church that he had felt a calling from God to save all people of South Africa, even though he knew he would be rejected by his own people."[4]

---

4   Philip Yancey, Whats so Amazing about Grace, Zondervan. 1997. p.36. and of course those like Nelson Mandela and Desmond Tutu had been working towards this for decades.

The darkness has never overcome the light, as we have it in John's Gospel (1:5).

As a modern translation puts it, "The life-light blazed out of the darkness; the darkness couldn't put it out." (Eugene Peterson, The Message, Nav Press 1995).

This light I understand as the love expressed supremely in the recorded words and attitude of Jesus of Nazareth from a cross and which has shone into the lives of human beings who have again and again followed the example of Jesus Christ in bringing this light into and out of darkness.

In this exploration, as in my previous book, I have found it necessary to paddle in the pool of the academics, to whom I am most grateful, together with all those too many to mention who have in the ordinary course of life expressed the light of that love which is eternal. An enigma, yes, because we can never fully explain it or get to the bottom of it, but an enigma which is the answer to the world's dilemma.

This love has been expressed to varying degrees in people who have known its source and those who have not. The most crucial thing for our world is that it be expressed in increasing measure. The Dalai Lama has written, "Love and compassion are most important, most precious, most powerful, and most sacred. Practising them is useful not only in terms of true religion, but also in worldly life for both mental and physical health. They are the basic elements supporting our life and happiness. With practice they become effective and beneficial driving forces for life."[5]

---

5   Widening the Circle of Love, His Holiness the Dalai Lama, Rider Publication, 2002 p.209

Dr Martin Luther King Jnr said, " ... So this morning, as I look into your eyes, and into the eyes of all of my brothers in Alabama and all over America and over the world, I say to you, I love you. I would rather die than hate you ... And I'm foolish enough to believe that through the power of this love somewhere, men of the most recalcitrant bent will be transformed. And then we will be in God's kingdom ... Oh God, help us in our lives and in all our attitudes to work out this controlling force of love, this controlling power that can solve every problem that we confront in all areas. Oh, we talk about politics; we talk about the problems facing our atomic civilisation. Grant that all men will come together and discover that as we solve the crisis and solve these problems – the international problems, the problems of atomic energy, the problems of nuclear energy, and yes, even the race problem – let us join together in a great fellowship of love and bow down at the feet of Jesus. Give us this strong determination. In the name and spirit of this Christ, we pray. Amen."[6]

In this work I shall quote extensively from a number of sources to highlight the importance of the practice of this kind of love, as expressed by Martin Luther King Jnr, and the Dalai Lama, Martin Buber, Tolstoy, William Barclay, and many others as will be seen in these pages. I will also see it as that which reaches beyond this present world into an eternity of being. There will be of course something of an overlap between the chapters due to the common

---

6   From a sermon delivered at Dexter Ave Baptist Church, Montgomery, Alabama, 17th Nov 1957, from The Great Sermons of Martin Luther King Jnr., Little Brown & Company 1999 pp.59-60

theme. One could in fact call this something of an anthology of love's attitudes, words and actions.

This love I am endeavouring to understand is 'down to earth and up to heaven'. It is practical; again Martin Luther King Jnr commenting on Jesus' words to love our enemies and our neighbours, says, "Certainly these are great words, words lifted to cosmic proportions. And over the centuries, many persons have argued that this is an extremely difficult command. Many would go so far as to say that it just isn't possible to move into the actual practice of this glorious command. They would go on to say that this is just additional proof that Jesus was an impractical idealist who never quite came down to earth. So the arguments abound. But far from being an impractical idealist, Jesus had become the practical realist. The words of this text glitter in our eyes with a new urgency. Far from being the pious injunction of a utopian dreamer, this command is an absolute necessity for the survival of our civilisation. Yes, it is love that will save our world and our civilisation, love even for enemies."[7]

Nelson Mandela put this into practice when, after some twenty seven years in prison, he had his jailer stand on his inauguration platform with him on being made President of South Africa. He was determined to break the cycle of revenge. It is this practical down to earth, up to heaven kind of love that we now set out to discover.

---

7   Ibid pp.41-42

Chapter 1.

Aspects of love

Is there any way of overcoming some of the obstacles which stand in the way of human progress? This question was once put to Bertrand Russell, the famous British philosopher, a prolific writer on religion, politics and morals. Though an atheist possibly agnostic, and critic of religion, he answered:

"What stands in the way? Not physical or technical obstacles, but only the evil passions in human minds; suspicion, fear, lust for power, intolerance ... the root of the matter is a very simple and old fashioned thing, a thing so simple that I am almost ashamed to mention it, for fear of the derisive smile with which wise cynics will greet my words. The thing I mean – please forgive me for mentioning it – is love, Christian love, or compassion ..."[8]

---

8   The Impact of Science on Society, Allen & Unwin, 1952 p.114 quoted in The Case for Christianity, Colin Chapman, Lion, 1981 p.22. Russell at different times during his life, admitted to being an atheist and agnostic

Bertrand Russell claimed that, "longing for love, the search for knowledge, and unbearable pity for mankind"[9] were the governing passions of his life.

Compassionate love is of course the ingredient that is vital for human relationships, and how Homo sapiens relate to the world, the cosmos, and the environment. One of the incomprehensible aspects of the enigma of love is in forgiveness, even for enemies. When this is expressed, miracles of understanding and forgiveness take place, the ingredients of peace. All that is good, all that seeks to heal relationships, all that seeks to break down animosity, all that breathes into our world the fresh air of forgiveness; all are aspects of this enigma of love of which we speak, and we shall see again and again aspects of love have come out of the most distressing of circumstances. Forgiveness is beautifully portrayed in this story from Enniskillen.

On Sunday 8th November 1987, Remembrance Day, a bomb went off at the Cenotaph in Enniskillen, Northern Ireland. There were serious casualties. A man named Gordon Wilson was one of those caught directly in the blast with his daughter, Marie; his daughter was killed.

In Northern Ireland the local BBC Radio news broadcast an interview with Gordon Wilson. He said ...

"The wall collapsed ... and we were thrown forward ... rubble and stones ... all around us and under us. I remember thinking ... 'I'm not hurt' ... but there's a pain in my shoulder ... I shouted to Marie, 'Are you alright?', and she said 'Yes' ... she found my hand and said, 'Is that your

---

9   Quoted in the Macmillan Encyclopaedia, 1981 p.1059

hand, Dad?' ... I said, 'Are you alright, dear?' ... but we were under six feet of rubble ... three or four times I asked her. She always said, 'Yes, I'm alright' ... I asked her the fifth time ... 'Are you alright, Marie?' ... She said, 'Daddy, I love you very much" ... those were the last words she spoke to me ... I kept shouting, 'Marie, are you alright?' ... there was no reply ... I have lost my daughter, but I bear no ill will; I bear no grudge ... Dirty sort of talk is not going to bring her back to life ... I don't have an answer ... but I know there has to be a plan. If I didn't think that, I would commit suicide ... it's part of a greater plan, and God is good ... and we shall meet again."[10]

Gordon Wilson was presented with the medal and ribbon of the 1988 World Methodist Peace Award. He concluded his speech with these words, "May I finish with the words of John Greenleaf Whittier, the New England poet and hymn writer, who says it all infinitely better than I could ever hope to do:

> Follow with reverent steps the great example
> Of him whose holy work was doing good;
> So shall the wide earth seem our Father's temple,
> Each loving life a psalm of gratitude.
>
> Then shall all shackles fall, the stormy clangour of wild
> war-music o'er the earth shall cease;
> Love shall tread out the baleful fire of anger,
> And in its ashes, plant the tree of peace.

Gordon Wilson quotes the words of Jesus and comments, 'A new commandment I give you, that you love one another.'

---

10 From 'Marie, a story from Enniskillen', Gordon Wilson with Alf McCreary, Marshall Pickering, 1990 p.xiv

That's basically it. Those words about love were burned into me by Marie's experience. Her last words were, 'Daddy, I love you very much'. She went out on words of love, and I have to stay on that plane. Hopefully and thankfully, with God's grace, I will keep on trying to do that ...

Marie showed that to us all, as she lay under the rubble at the Cenotaph holding my hand, with her life slipping away. The bottom line is love. There's nothing more I can say."[11]

We note that Bertrand Russell(atheist or agnostic) still believed in love, and yearned for it, together with a great compassion for humanity and a yearning for knowledge, which I think we could fairly interpret as longing for truth. And we have another man who even in the face of great cruelty and disaster, in the face of man's inhumanity to man, believes in love, such love that it enables him to live in the present with a belief in life that transcends this earthly scene, a love that unites him for ever with his daughter, a love that has an eternal dimension to it, and a love that promotes peace in this world when it is responded to and expressed in lived lives.

Bertrand Russell and Gordon Wilson, you could say, were poles apart in background and education, but they were one in recognising that love, this understanding of love or compassion is the key to life, that which alone is the answer to evil passions, suspicion, fear, lust for power, intolerance. This love alone is the key to peace within and without, peace individually and universally; it is this which gives meaning, purpose and salvation, even if Bertrand Russell did not recognise the source, can we not say that the love he sought was his salvation.

---

11   Ibid p,121

I hope during this work we shall begin to see that this love transcends prejudice, culture, colour, religion, belief and unbelief; this love does conquer and will ultimately be victorious over hate and all that would destroy life. This love is that which enhances life, it creates and recreates; this I contend is the very source of life.

As noted earlier the early Christians, wanting to find a word to describe the kind of love that Jesus Christ embodied and ultimately expressed on the cross, used a word not much in use at that time; other words of love could not bring out its special quality which they wished to express, and so agape came to be used; love that included the crucial ingredient, 'grace', undeserved favour.

This is the love that removes bitterness and allows one the freedom to live. This is the love Gordon Wilson expressed; the new commandment to love that Jesus gave to his disciples had this element of grace, so beautifully portrayed in the recorded words of Jesus from the cross, "Father, forgive them, they know not what they do." Jesus Christ proclaimed the love he preached with his own body from a cross, agape: the Buddhist monk Thich Nhat Hanh understanding this wrote, "Love meditation is not wishful thinking, it is an authentic practice."[12]

Miracles occur when this love is activated to a remarkable degree; as in a case recorded by the Truth and Reconciliation

12 Essential writings – Ed Sister Annabel Laity, Orbis, 2001 p.104. Reprinted from the Teachings on Love(1998) by Tich Nhat Hanh with permission of Parallax Press,Berkeley,California,www.Parallax. org reprinted from the Teachings on Love(1998) by Tich Nhat Hanh with permission of Parallax Press,Berkeley,California,www.Parallax. org

Commission set up in South Africa by Nelson Mandela and Archbishop Desmond Tutu ,...in the court ...

"A frail black woman stands slowly to her feet. She is something over 70 years of age. Facing her from across the room are a number of white security police officers. One, a Mr Van der Broek, has just been tried and found implicated in the murders of the woman's son and husband some years before. It was in fact Mr Van der Broek, it was now established, who had come to the woman's home, taken her son and shot him at point-blank range, and then burned the young man's body on a fire while he and his fellow officer partied nearby.

Several years later, Mr Van der Broek and his officers returned to take away her husband as well. For many months she heard nothing of his whereabouts.

Then, almost two years after her husband had been taken, Mr Van der Broek came back to fetch the woman herself. How vividly she remembers that evening, going down to a place beside the river, where she was shown her husband, bound and beaten, but strong in spirit. He lay on a pile of wood. The last words she heard from his lips as the officers poured gasoline over his body and set him on fire were, "Father, forgive them."

And now this dear lady stands in the courtroom and listens to the confessions given by Mr Van der Broek. A member of South Africa's Truth and Reconciliation Commission turns to her and asks, "So what do you want? How should justice be done to this man who has so brutally destroyed your family?"

"I want three things" the woman says calmly, confidently, "I want first to be taken to the place where my husband's body was burned so that I can gather up the dust and give his remains a decent burial."

She pauses, and then continues, "My husband and son were my only family. I want, secondly, therefore, for Mr Van der Broek to become my son. I would like for him to come twice a month to the ghetto and spend a day with me so that I can pour out on him whatever love I still have remaining in me."

"And finally" she says, "I want a third thing. I would like Mr Van der Broek to know that I offer him my forgiveness because Jesus Christ died to forgive. This was also the wish of my husband. And so, I would kindly ask someone to come to my side and lead me across this courtroom so that I can take Mr Van der Broek in my arms, embrace him, and let him know that he is truly forgiven."

As the courtroom assistants come to lead the elderly woman across the room, Mr Van der Broek, overwhelmed by what he has just heard, faints, and as he does so, those in the courtroom, friends, family, neighbours – all victims of decades of oppression and injustice – begin to sing softly but assuredly, 'Amazing grace, how sweet the sound that saved a wretch like me.'[13]

The love Jesus of Nazareth expressed in his ministry broke down the cultural and ethnic barriers we sometimes set up. It breaks down animosity and brings a message of

---

13   Quoted from 'Spring Harvest' Study Guide, by Jeff Lucas, 2001 p.47

reconciliation. He broke down the narrow prejudices of his own day. Jesus cites as an example of compassion the story of the Good Samaritan.

Jesus sets a Samaritan up as an example of love in action. Those who kept traditions, religious rules and regulations to the exclusion of compassion, walked by on the other side when they saw a man broken and injured lying in the road. The Samaritan stops to bind up his wounds and supplies the monetary means for ongoing care. This Samaritan was a member of a mixed race, and he would not have regarded the whole of the scriptures (The Old Testament) as the word of God as the Jews did. The Samaritans only accepted the first five books of Moses, the Pentateuch, excluding the rest of the Old Testament. The Samaritans were regarded as schismatics.

Jesus in this parable makes it clear that the expression of love (compassion) is above any dogmatic creeds. Although Jesus himself was a Jew, his love breached religious and ethnic prejudices; class and religious ceremonial practices were subordinate to love (agape). It is true that certain rules, religious traditions can indeed be helpful, but when they exclude compassion, they become a barrier. St Paul makes the point well when he states, "The entire law is summed up in a single command, love your neighbour as yourself (Galatians 5:14); he has made us competent as ministers of a new covenant – not of the letter but of the spirit; for the letter kills, but the spirit gives life." (2 Corinthians 3:6); or we could say, rules without compassion are dead!

In Genesis in the Bible it says man is made in the image of God (spirit). So we can say humanity originated from the spirit – which is compassion, agape love; understanding this from the equation:-

From the Bible, John 4:24 "God is Spirit" and in 1 John 4:16 "God is love; whoever lives in love lives in God and God in him." So, God = Spirit. Spirit = Love, agape, compassion.[14]

This element in the human make up does rise to the surface again and again; this spirit of compassion rooted in agape love, this desire for peace, breaking down of animosities. It is significant that the story of the birth of Jesus should give birth to a making of peace in the First World War for a brief spell on the Western front.

This aspect of love which is peace and reconciliation was demonstrated again and again because Christmas was honoured. Enemies would be shaking hands, exchanging gifts, sharing family photographs. It was felt by opposing forces that this season of the year should be honoured by a truce, and it happened even in the midst of the horrors of war. I believe these accounts have their foundations in a stream of creative love evident throughout history implicit if not explicit in all such circumstances.

There are a number of well documented accounts of the Christmas truce that took place on the Western Front in 1914-15 to the extent that two thirds kept a Christmas and even New Year's truce, not ordered by the High Commands on either side, but taking place on the initiative of ordinary soldiers in the trenches.

---

14   This is expanded in more detail in my book 'Hell – Fact or Fiction?', Athena Press, 2006 p.60

The Crown Prince Wilhelm of Prussia, son of the Kaiser, the Commander of the German Fifth Army in the Argonne region, which had seen fierce fighting throughout this first winter of the war, visited the front line; he records:

"... Every dugout had its Christmas tree, and from all directions came the sound of rough men's voices singing our exquisite old Christmas songs. Kirchhoff, the concert singer, who was attached to our headquarters staff for a while as orderly officer, sang his Christmas songs on that same sacred evening in the frontline trenches of the 130th Regiment. And on the following day he told me that some French soldiers who had climbed up their parapet had continued to applaud, until at last he gave them an encore. Thus, amid the bitter realities of trench warfare, with all its squalor, a Christmas song had worked a miracle and thrown a bridge from man to man ..."[15]

Under the title 'Christmas Peace 1914 at the Flanders Front', a German magazine published an account of a remarkable burial service written in response to an English account, written twenty years after the event by a Major Thomas, instructor at the infantry school Dresden.

"... We heard that it was the wish of the Englishman to bury on the occasion of the Christmas holiday their dead who were lying before the front ... there was no time for making enquiries of the superior department ... Commander Baron Von Bomberg, cousin of the Reich Defence Minister, decided without anything further that there should be a local armistice. ...

---

15 'The Christmas Truce', Malcolm Brown & Shirley Seaton, Pan Books, 2001 p.75

… Our Padre … arranged the prayers and psalm etc. and an interpreter wrote them out in German. They were read first in English by our padre, and then in German by a boy who was studying for the ministry. It was an exciting and most wonderful sight. The Germans formed up on one side, the English on the other, the officers standing in front, every head bared. Yes, I think it was a sight one will never see again. Standing between the ranks of British and German officers, Chaplain Esslemont Adams spoke the familiar words of the 23rd Psalm The Lord is my Shepherd.

As the service came to an end there was a moment of silence, then the chaplain stepped forward and saluted the German commander, who shook hands with him and bade him farewell. 'It was an impressive sight', the regimental history of the 6/Gordons recorded, 'Officers and men, bitter enemies as they were, uncovered, and for the moment united in offering for their dead the last office of homage and honour.'[16]

A German soldier wrote, "It was a Christmas celebration in keeping with the command 'Peace on earth', and a memory which will stay with us always"[17].

Bruce Bairn's father wrote, 'there was not an atom of hate on either side that day'…

In view of the horrors which have followed, it would be easy to dismiss the events of that far off Christmas as little more than a candle in the darkness. Yet they offer a light where no light might have been, and are thus a

---

16   Ibid, pp.89-90

17   Ibid, p.93

source of encouragement and hope that should not be over-looked and forgotten, rather acknowledged and, indeed, celebrated."[18]

As an example of compassion we have the account given by Harry Patch in 2007, the last soldier to have fought in the trenches of the First World War, describing the attitude of the Lewis Gun team of which he was a part –

"The team was very close-knit and it had a pact. It was this: Bob said we wouldn't kill, not if we could help it. He said, 'We fire short, have them in the legs, or fire over their heads, but not to kill, unless it was them or us.'"

Harry Patch gave this view of that war – "By the time I was demobbed I was thoroughly disillusioned. I could never understand why my country could call me from a peace-time job and train me to go out to France and try to kill a man I never knew. Why did we fight? I asked myself that many times. At the end of the war, the peace was settled round a table, so why the hell couldn't they do that at the start, without losing millions of men?"[19]

More lights in the darkness were to be seen in the concentration camps of the Second World War.

"In Auschwitz where hunger and hatred reigned, and faith evaporated, Maximilian Kolbe opened his heart to others and spoke of God's infinite love. He never seemed to think of himself. When food was brought in, and everyone struggled to get a place in the queue to be sure of his share,

18   Ibid. p.93 & 215-216

19   'The Last Fighting Tommy', Harry Patch with Richard Van Eden, Bloomsbury, 2007, Paperback, 2008 p.71 & p.137

Maximilian stood aside, so that frequently there was none for him. At other times he shared his meagre ration of soup and bread with others. He once told another priest, 'We must be grateful we are here. There is so much for us to do; look how people need us.'"[20]

Finally he took the place of another in the death block and ministered hope and comfort even there, bringing worship and prayer in place of despair.

Another light in the darkness was Maria Skobtsova a nun in Ravensbruck concentration camp.

"Her robust constitution, wide ranging interests and habit of prayer, saved her from being utterly disoriented by the conditions prevailing in Ravensbruck. Others were not so fortunate. There, in the camp, human misery and suffering were taken to breaking point. At three each morning the women had to stand out in the open in all weathers, until everyone had been counted, a procedure (known as the Appel) that regularly took five or more hours. Maria took it calmly; many could not. Maria would not succumb to despair. 'Whatever you do' she begged then 'continue to think. Don't allow the flame of your spirit to die. In conflict with doubt, cast your thoughts wider and deeper. Do not let your thoughts be debased. Let it transcend the conditions and limitations of this earth.' …

A survivor said, 'We were cut off from our families; yet somehow she provided us with a family.'

---

20   Quoted in my book 'Hell – Fact or Fiction?', Athena Press, 2006 p.23. From 'Saints of the 20th Century', Brother Kenneth, CGA, Mowbrays, 1976 pp.97-98

… Maria was mother to them all, but particularly to the young Soviet women soldiers in Block 31 whom she adopted as her own, hugging them like children when they were afraid."[21]

We notice that she held out eternal hope for all, for Soviet young women soldiers, who, coming from an atheist state, presumably held no belief in God. In fact, she had a special place in her heart for them.

We notice that Dietrich Bonhoeffer, German pastor and theologian, would not take a service for inmates of his prison while a devout communist was excluded. They had gone through so much together as a group, and he did not want any to feel left out. It was not until the man himself came to Bonhoeffer (without any pressure) asking to be included, that he agreed to take the service.

Bonhoeffer preached from Isaiah 53:5, Peter's Epistle and John's Gospel.

Payne Best remembers: 'he reached the hearts of us all, finding just the right words to express the spirit of our imprisonment, and the thoughts and resolutions which it had brought.' (While the men were reflecting on his words, he was taken away to be executed. … leaving a whispered message for Payne Best for his old friend, Bishop Bell. 'Tell him,' he said, 'that for me this is the end, but also the beginning'.[22]

During his imprisonment and right up to the end,

---

21 Ibid. From 'Candles in the Dark', Mary Craig (Spire), Hodder, 1984 pp.240-241

22 Ibid p. 54

Bonhoeffer was ministering to others seeking to bring hope and encouragement. I would maintain the love he sought to express was of that eternal quality that not even impending death could destroy. It was the same almighty power that Maximilian Kolbe exercised when he opened his heart to others, and even in the death block expressed that infinite love.In the midst of suffering there was that which was greater than hate, that which gave hope even to those who knew they were dying, but the love that Maximilian Kolbe and Maria Skobtsova, expressed gave such hope for an eternal future, it enabled life to be lived in the present. It is the love that overcame hate on that cross so long ago, that love that does not keep a record of wrongs, that love that even with feelings of forsakenness is the very power of new life, of resurrection.

This love gives strength for the present, and hope for eternal future. Here is another aspect of love.

"The Abbey of Our Lady of the Arlas lies in a small village called Tibhirine, about sixty miles south of Algiers. In the early 90's civil war broke out between the government and the G.I.A. In 1993 an ultimatum was given by the G.I.A. that all foreigners must leave by the 1st December under pain of death.

After agreeing three should leave, nine stayed. They did so out of love for Algeria ... "especially out of love for their Muslim neighbours, with whom they had excellent relations; the villagers were also being terrorised and saw the presence of the monks as reassurance. In the absence of a village mosque, the villagers had the use of a room in the monastery for prayer, and the monks and villagers together ran a market garden ..."

In a letter to Fr Christian another monk described their task: 'that in our day to day relations, we should openly be on the side of love, forgiveness and communion, against hate, vengeance and violence.' By having death daily before their eyes, their lives took on a new energy of love ... then, one night in March 1996, gunmen arrived and abducted Fr Christian and six other monks. A month later an ultimatum was issued to the Algerian government: free all GIA prisoners or the monks would have their throats slit. In May the threat was carried out, and the seven Arlas Martyrs joined the growing number of Christians who had given their lives out of love for their Muslim neighbours ..."

Fr Christian had written a letter or testament to be opened in the event of his death. In this letter his final words were for his executioner ... "and also you, my last-minute friend, who will not have known what you were doing: yes, I want this thank you and this adieu to be for you too, because in God's face I see yours. May we meet again as happy thieves in paradise, if it pleases God, the father of us both. Amen! Inch Allah!'"

Abbot Christofer Jamison, who gives us this account of the Arlas martyrs, comments "For Fr Christian death was the supreme moment of love ... for the Arlas Martyrs, death was the final expression of the faith, hope and love that had filled their lives."[23]

We have the recorded words of Jesus of Nazareth 'to love our neighbours as ourselves'. Jesus went on to illustrate

---

23 This account comes from 'Finding Sanctuary, Monastic Steps for Everyday Life', from the TV series 'The Monastery', BBC, Phoenix, 2007

this with the story of the Good Samaritan which we have already noted; where compassion is shown to a member of another race regarded as an enemy; Jesus' words, 'love your enemies' do not mean we condone the wrongs that are done, but endeavour to seek the best for all concerned, as well as ourselves, including those regarded as enemies.

The Buddhist monk Thich Nhat Hanh has written on this crucial subject. The Baptist minister Dr Martin Luther King Jnr, the great civil rights campaigner, wrote of Thich Nhat Hanh, "I do not personally know of anyone more worthy of the Noble Peace Prize than this gentle Buddhist monk from Vietnam ... his ideas for peace, if applied, would build a monument to ecumenism, to world brotherhood, to humanity."

Thich Nhat Hanh has written:

"When our practice has become solid and we are able to understand love and care for ourselves, at least to some extent, we can make others the object of our love meditation; then, successively, someone neutral to us, someone we love, and someone we dislike very much.

During the Vietnamese War, I meditated on the Vietnamese soldiers, praying they would not be killed in battle. But I also meditated on the American soldiers and felt a very deep sympathy for them. I knew that they had been sent far away from home to kill or be killed, and I prayed for their safety. That led to a deep aspiration that the war would end and allow Vietnamese and Americans to live in peace. Once that aspiration was clear, there was only one path to take – to work for the end of the war.

When you practise love meditation, you have to take that path."[24]

A veteran told him his platoon had nearly all been wiped out by guerrillas; the survivors were so angry they made cookies with explosives in them, they left them on the side of the road – some children came along and ate them, the explosives went off.

"They were rolling around the ground in pain. Their parents tried to save their lives, but there was nothing they could do. That image of the children rolling on the ground dying because of the explosives in the cookies was so deeply ingrained on this veteran's heart, that now, twenty years later, he still could not sit in the same room with children. He was living in hell. After he had told his story, I gave him the practice of Beginning Anew.

Beginning Anew is not easy. We have to transform our hearts and our minds in very practical ways. We may feel ashamed, but shame is not enough to change our heart. I said to him, 'You killed five or six children that day? Can you save the lives of five or six children today? Children everywhere in the world are dying because of war, malnutrition, and disease. You keep thinking about the five or six children that you killed in the past, but what about the children who are dying now? You still have your body, you still have your heart, and you can do many things to help

---

24   Essential Writings, Sister Annabel Laity, Orbis, 2001 pp.103-104. Reprinted from the teachings on Love(1998) by Tich Nhat Hanh with permission of Parallax Press,Berkeley,California,www.Parallax. org reprinted from the teachings on Love(1998) by Tich Nhat Hanh with permission of Parallax Press,Berkeley,California,www.Parallax. org

children who are dying in the present moment. Please give rise to your mind of love, and in the months and years that are left to you, do the work of helping children.' He agreed to do it, and it has helped him transform his guilt."[25]

In the love of agape we are never in a position to 'go it alone', though this may be what is felt in times of darkness; in a dark twisting tunnel in the middle the light can't be seen but It is there all the time.And in our understanding of this love it is even there in the deepest darkness. Thich Nhat Hanh revealed the light of love to this veteran and introduced him to a community of compassion – of putting right that which was wrong through changing the present and the future, by putting into practice the love he had received, in pouring out this love to children in need.

Thich Nhat Hanh observed, "When we look into and touch deeply the life and teaching of Jesus, we can penetrate the reality of God. Love, understanding, courage, and acceptance are expressions of the life of Jesus. God made Himself known to us through Jesus Christ ... for me, the life of Jesus is his most basic teaching, more important than even faith in the resurrection or faith in eternity."[26]

We owe much to the writings of this gracious monk, but there is also within the concept of agape love the crucial importance of resurrection as being together with the crucifixion the peak of the supreme importance of love as seen in the term agape.

In 1 Corinthians 13:13 we read love is greater than faith;

---

25   Ibid. pp.107-108

26   Ibid. pp.139-140

and the crucial truth is that resurrection is the fruit of love, it is also crucial that there is an eternal dimension where love puts right all wrongs; where injustices are corrected, for it is obvious this is not always the case in this temporal life (we shall explore this further in the chapter on resurrection).

From a Christian perspective the love seen in the healing ministry of Jesus is ultimately seen in the victory over hate on the cross. Love's eternal everlasting quality is seen in its victory in and over death. Love can be appreciated in many ways, but in the sense of agape, cannot be fully appreciated without love's victory in death and resurrection. It is the action of this love in word, attitude and deed in the present and beyond (eternity) that opens up an understanding of life on an ever-increasing scale. It can be seen that the love that Jesus expressed and supremely declared on the cross and in resurrection is a love that is recognized in different cultures and religions, and in those of no religion. This love is expressed, as we have seen, in all kinds of circumstances; it is expressed across all ethnic barriers, whenever compassion is activated the liberating power of love is experienced It gives assurance, consolation, reconciliation, challenge, comfort, peace, in so many different ways, in so many circumstances, but all ways that bring new beginnings, new understanding of life, all ways that build up and enable people to live.

It is the understanding of love as defined by Jesus of Nazareth that inspired such attitudes and actions in such as Martin Luther King Jnr of the Civil Rights Movement, reaching out in love even to his enemies, Mahatma Ghandi to reach out to people of all faiths with compassion and understanding and to express love even to enemies, Maximilian Kolbe to transform the death block into a place of prayer and hope, giving renewed life even in the face of death, William Wilberforce who was the mainspring behind the abolition of the slave trade in 18th century England; it was this love that prompted Thich Nhat Hanh to bring healing to the traumatised in the Vietnam war. It was this understanding of love that gave birth to the founding of the Truth and Reconciliation Commission in South Africa led by Nelson Mandela and Archbishop Desmond Tutu, which cut the cycle of revenge and concentrated on forgiveness and reconciliation and new beginnings in compassion. And love shown by Fr. Christian and his monks, and love shown by Moslems and Christians living in harmony, in communion.

Although the church and religion have been rightly criticised for its failures in compassion, there is another side to the story. History shows how people have been blessed again and again in our world due to the good influence of religion and the church on their lives. It has been the seedbed for a multitude of acts of compassion.

The following are more examples of so many more that could be given.

Albert Schweitzer with his medical work in Lambarene in Africa, Elizabeth Fry with her work in prison reform, Mother Teresa with her work among the destitute and dying, Doctor Cecily Saunders who founded the modern hospice movement, Group Captain Leonard Cheshire, a World War II veteran set up an organisation for the disabled, which is now worldwide, Jean Henri Dunant who was the inspiration for founding the Red Cross movement, and so one could go on and on. And in our own time we have no end of churches and organisations who bless local people, set up social care programmes, in a wide range of projects, such as Steve Chalke founder of oasis trust and stop the traffic. Plus helping all kinds of people through all kinds of problems, plus giving a dimension of life so vast it includes temporal and eternal aspects of living. None of the pioneers for good were perfect of course, but the amount of good they generated has blessed the world in their own time and beyond. Whenever Jesus' understanding of love is responded to and explored, both by those of religious affiliation and those without, beautiful things happen.

It has become popular for a number of writers to home in on the down side of the church's history, ignoring the good, writers such as Richard Dawkins, Philip Pullman, Peter Atkins, Stephen Hawking, Carl Sagan, etc. One of Richard Dawkins' statements proclaims, "I do not believe there is an atheist in the world who would bulldoze Mecca or Chartres, York Minster, or Notre Dame.'

Alistair McGrath comments, "Sadly this noble sentiment is a statement about his personal credulity, not the reality of things ... the history of the Soviet Union is replete with the burning and dynamiting of huge numbers of churches. His pleading that atheism is innocent of violence and oppression that he associates with religion is simply untenable, and suggests a significant blind spot."[27]

Alistair McGrath goes on to give an illustration from the study by the Oxford scholar Alexandra Popescu of the

---

27   Quoted in 'The Dawkins Delusion?', SPCK, 2007 p.48

Rumanian Christian dissident intellectual Petre Tutea (1902-91).

"... Alexandra Popescu documents the physical and mental degradation Tutea suffered as part of systematic persecution of religion in Rumania during the Soviet era until the downfall and execution of Nicolae Ceausescu. During this period Tutea spent thirteen years as a prisoner of conscience, and twenty eight years under house arrest. His personal story is enormously illuminating for those who want to understand the power of religious faith to console and maintain personal identity under precisely the forms of persecution that Dawkins believes do not exist."[28]

The power of this love is indeed paradoxical, power in weakness, power in powerlessness, power that kept Tutea during his ordeal.

There is something that cannot be put down to the functions of genes. There is that which operates in life that the early Christians described as agape, compassion of a remarkable nature.

"You will have heard of Oskar Schindler because he has been made famous by a book and a film about him. He saved many Jews from the Nazis.

Sendlerova saved many more -2500 children and babies – and her awe-inspiring bravery has gone unrecognised until relatively recently. By the time you read these words it is possible that she will have been awarded the Nobel Peace Prize. There can scarcely be a worthier winner ...

---

28 Ibid. pp.48-49, from Alexandru D. Popescu, Petre Tutea: Between Sacrifice and Suicide, Aldershot, Ashgate, 2004

She was a social worker in Poland when the Nazis invaded and methodically set about trying to murder every Jewish man, woman and child. In 1940 they established the famous Warsaw Ghetto, isolating the 380,000 Jews in the city. The intention was that all those who did not die of starvation or disease, or were too sick, old or young to work, would be shipped off to the concentration camps.

Mrs Sendlerova, who was not yet thirty years old, organised a small group of social workers to smuggle Jewish children to safety. She did not know the children she saved. She did not share their religion or their race. They were strangers to her in every sense, but she did it anyway. Not just once: this was no impulsive act of mercy. It was not like seeing a child fall into a lake and jumping in to rescue her – or even stepping into the path of a machete-swinging madman to save the children in your care. This was calculated, repeated over and over again."[29]

With every child spirited out of the hell of the Warsaw Ghetto, rescued from the unimaginable horror of the Nazi death camps, she moved a step closer to her own capture. And in the end – as it was bound to – it happened. She was caught by the Gestapo and savagely beaten, both legs and feet broken, then taken away to be murdered. Mercifully, she was saved by partisans and lived a full life. And not once did she boast about what she had done or demand recognition. Her awe-inspiring story remained virtually untold until she was an old woman, almost half a century after the war had ended. In an interview at the age of ninety-seven she said:

---

29 'In God We Doubt, Confessions of a Failed Atheist', Hodder, 2007 p.p.266-267

"I was brought up to believe that a person must be rescued when drowning, regardless of religion and nationality. The term 'hero' irritates me greatly. The opposite is true. I continue to have pangs of conscience that I did so little."

It may be scientifically plausible to talk of primitive 'urges' and 'misfirings' and of 'Darwinian mistakes'. It may be that she saved the lives of 2500 children because, as Dawkins might put it, she simply 'could not help herself.'...

... But I don't believe that. I believe she did it because she was a good woman blessed with a capacity for pure, *unselfish love* and a conscience that would not allow her to behave in any other way. She was a truly virtuous woman. And it raises that troubling question: if we dismiss all notion of a divine spark, why did she do it?"[30]

What moved this woman is what we have called the light, the silver lining in life, it's that compassion born of that love which is eternal, unselfish love – agape.

And John Humphrys quotes and comments on words from the 2nd Vatican Council ...

"In the depth of his conscience, man detects a law which he does not impose upon himself, but which holds him in obedience, always summoning him to love good and avoid evil ... conscience is the most secret core and sanctuary of a man. There he is: alone with God, whose voice echoes in his depths ....

... there is that other mysterious attribute, about which so many scientists are curiously incurious. There is our

---

30   Ibid. pp.268-269

soul, our spirit, our conscience or whatever else you want to call it."[31]

Prince Charles addressing psychiatrists about their work spoke eloquently on behalf of patients. "I believe that the most urgent need for western man is to rediscover that divine element in his being, without which there never can be any possible hope or meaning to our existence in this earthly realm."[32]

This is the spirit that responds to this love (compassion) suffusing light and hope in the darkness. It is a fact that there have always been that host of people who to a lesser or greater degree, some known, some unknown to the world at large, who have spread the light of love, some will include neighbours, friends, family, who have been lights for us in our dark moments. Such as two prison visitors who brought light and hope into the dark world of a young inmate who had lost all hope.

Let me share this account given by one of those visitors on his visit this year (2008).

"One case that will be ever etched in my memory is when we were called in by an officer to the segregation unit. A prisoner had been crying and the officers had tried to talk with him but were unable to make a break through. The lady who I had trained with came with me, his cell was opened by the officer, we went in and sat at his invitation either side of him on his bed.

---

31   Ibid. p.280

32   1991 150th Anniversary British Journal of Psychiatry, 159-763-768, quoted in 'Is Faith a Delusion?' p.9

He was totally distraught, and continued to sob. We asked if he would talk to just one of us, but no response came. The officer called us out and told us we were wasting our time. Just then the lady said, 'I have an idea.' back we went into the cell, she then held his hand and made him look at her. She, in a very calm voice, said to him, 'We love you and want to help you'. With that he just collapsed into sobbing. I pleaded with him just to give us a clue.

Eventually he spoke and asked us, 'Do you really care and love me?' we said, 'Yes'.

He then, between sobs, told us he had never known a real home, he was placed in foster homes around the country, never allowed to settle, when he started to make friends he was moved on. He ran away many times, skipped school, this pattern was his life until he left school. He eventually got into drugs, he made what he called friends because they looked after him, and it was the first time in his life that anyone had taken an interest in him.

He was caught many times and did small sentences, eventually he was sentenced for six years, and was due to be sent to an open prison to adapt him for life outside, but admitted he was scared. The bombshell came when he turned and looked at us and told us we were the first people in his life to tell him he was loved. He was twenty seven years of age.

Probation became heavily involved and did an excellent job before he left for the open prison. The Chaplain promised to visit, and reported that he had found a totally different man who was so grateful that someone had taken the time to listen to him. The feelings we had when we got back to the office of being elated but utterly drained stayed with us for days. In our conversation with the Chaplain later we discovered how our Lord must have felt when he knew tiredness, and when the woman who had the issue of blood touched Him and He knew that something had gone out from Him. In this day and age we need to be aware that lots of people need HOPE, and sometimes it is by listening to them that we can on occasion help them see a way forward."[33]

This young man was given hope, given life, because he was given love. This was given by two prison visitors whose names the world at large will never know. They brought to that young man the answer to his life's questions, love.

It is an undeniable fact that this love is expressed all the time, in good times and bad times. Without expressions of such love the world would be a dark place indeed, but as it is, and as an observable fact, as we have seen is tried and tested in all manner of circumstances, this love works again and again. Not always removing the obstacles and questions, but moving through the complexities of life. This I believe is the answer to living life to the full in this world; it is love's answers to life's questions that is the silver lining in life, and the most important element by far.

We have observed that in the most vulnerable of circumstances, even the most vulnerable of people bring hope. This love brings hope and life in temporal and eternal terms. I would maintain this love finds its roots in the kind of love Jesus of Nazareth expressed from a cross,

---

33   Account given to me by prison visitor. Phil Arnold, by kind permission

in all his vulnerability; out of that agony he would bring resurrection. He would bring life of such magnitude not even death would be able to annihilate it.

In our next chapter we shall attempt to explore the nature of this love which gives hope and life even in vulnerability, wholeness out of fragmentation.

Chapter 2.

Vulnerability and love

The power of military might, of muscle power, of political or economic power, do not of themselves produce life of such quality that it gives meaning, value and purpose to lives that are shattered by suffering of mind, body or spirit. What we are exploring gives faith to the faithless, love to the loveless, hope to the hopeless, and life to the lifeless. There are no end of accounts, of which we have looked at a mere handful, which declare how the power of love (compassion, agape,) is victorious in vulnerability.

This power of vulnerability leads one to investigate the source.

In many writings God is described in terms of attributes such as justice, love, mercy, knowledge, power, etc. but not so many describe what God is. What is G.O.D.?

I think this is most important for our understanding, even to a limited degree, of suffering, of love, human destiny and the universe.

We do not know the shape, size, make up of what we call 'God', the creator, 'the Real', 'the ground of all being', etc. In the Christian tradition 'God' is not depicted as an enlarged being like an animal, or a mixture of animal and human as in many religions, nor as some kind of divine super-being like the Greek and Roman gods.

"God is not a very powerful invisible superman, ...God is the one in whom no one is on the edge because God's centre is everywhere, and his circumference is nowhere. It is in the spaciousness of God that we will be completely at home because everyone will be."[34] ... God could well be beyond, above, around and within the universe, permeating the whole, bigger than the universe, but within it as well. This energy, this essence, 'The Real' as John Hick describes it[35], being the very light of life, as John in his Gospel describes, Christ the living word.

This creative energy creates out of its very vulnerable make up; bringing life out of darkness and chaos. This energy can also be seen in spiritual terms, as Spirit, as we read in Genesis, "In the beginning God created the heavens and the earth. Now the earth was formless and empty, darkness was over the face of the deep ... And the Spirit of God was hovering over the waters. And God said let there be light, and there was light ..." (Genesis 1:1-3)

The whole universe is seen as coming forth from fragmentation from a formless mass. Light and life from a

34 Seven Last Words, Timothy Radcliffe, Burns & Oats, Continuum, 2006 p.73 & What is the Point of Being a Christian?, Burns & Oates, 2005 pp.130-131. Reproduced by kind permission of Continuum International Publishing Group. Reproduced by kind permission of Continuum International Publishing Group.

35 The Fifth Dimension, John Hick, One World, 1999 p.9

diversification of elements; out of such vulnerability burst forth a diversity of chemical dust that would produce life, as we know it on earth. John Polkinghorne, one time professor of mathematical physics at Cambridge writes, … "The universe as we know it today emerged from the fiery singularity of the big bang … only because the laws of nuclear physics are what they are and no different, has the range of chemical elements necessary for carbon-based life been produced by the stars, from whose *dead ashes* we and all living creatures here on earth are made.

… Although the universe appears to have been lifeless for the first eleven billion years of its existence, there is a real sense in which it was pregnant with the possibility of life from the very beginning. Only because the balance between the fundamental forces of gravity and electromagnetism is what it is and no different have stars been able to burn for the billions of years that are necessary, if they are to be able to fuel the development of life on one of their planets."[36]

Thus it can be said as an established scientific observation life is vulnerable, that is obvious, and new life is produced out of that very vulnerability. It can also be stated as an observable fact that goodness, compassion, etc. is produced in the vulnerable even within and out of suffering, beautiful attitudes, acts, have taken place repeatedly.

It is logical that a humanity that is made in the image of its creator should exhibit some traits of that creator. (Genesis 1:26 'Then God said let us make man in our image …') Thus it follows that if we accept the hypothesis that the

---

36   The God of Hope and the End of the World, pp.4-5,15

creator is vulnerable, and that is where real power comes from, then one would expect this to be seen in humanity.

So we could say – God (the creator) = creative energy which is released in vulnerability, this vulnerability can be understood to be in fact the love of the universe, that again and again brings life out of death. And so in the image of the creator we do indeed see life coming out of death, light out of darkness, power out of apparent weakness. We have seen this in people in the concentration camps, those who brought in light, life, and renewed hope, in people like Dietrich Bonhoeffer, Maximillian Kolbe, Maria Skobtsove, etc.

Again and again humanity has produced those who have manifested the characteristics of their creator. Releasing more of the energy of that love, called in the New Testament agape, compassion, grace (undeserved favour). This is expressed in creative attitudes and acts. It is expressed in death and in life; no circumstance is a barrier to it when this love, this energy is released, not even death is a barrier. After all, John Polkinghorne informs us life came out of death i.e. the ashes of dead stars! There is a principle in creation of life coming forth from death.

Jesus Christ on the cross in all that vulnerability is described in John's Gospel as the 'word', the logos (John 1:1). Seen as the living embodiment of creative love, coming into the world as one of the most vulnerable forms of life, a human baby, living among the poor, reaching out to the disadvantaged, then dying on a cross, the ultimate vulnerability; yet even here we observe forgiveness pouring forth as John records the words of Jesus from the cross – love overcoming all the powers of hate, misunderstanding, revenge, returning love for hate. This is power, the power that can save the world, the power of life over death, resurrection out of dissolution.

Jesus of Nazareth even in the midst of the worst kind of desolation, cries out the 'why' question, releasing the saving energy of love, to all enemies as well as friends and family. Then in actual death, love's victory over humanity's final enemy – death is defeated. His body died, his spirit given up; and out of disintegration came new life in resurrection.

Now love (compassion) is generally recognised by all Homo sapiens as important for life, but it is not always seen as the absolute key, that opens up life to meaning, purpose and eternity.

However far-fetched it may sound, the understanding of God as the creator who is vulnerable love – the energy that creates life, and enables fullness of life in present living, has much to say about the problem of suffering. This love can be seen as an answer to the problems of suffering, not of course revealing the full answer now, due to our limited intelligence and availability of all the facts of life in the universe. But this understanding of vulnerable love can be seen as the key to the problem; while we do not at present know how the key opens the door fully (with all its questions) we can go as far as to say, we have begun to discover how to put the key into the lock!

So this vulnerable love, which is so creative and which paradoxically is real power can be seen as an answer to suffering in creation, and the seedbed of hope in hopelessness. This creative love I maintain is no fairy tale illusion, but in fact, is in operation every day in the lives of ordinary people in the nitty gritty of life; what I am suggesting is that which is seen in dealing with real life situations now, has far reaching significance even to pointing to the ultimate source of creation which gives this creation meaning, purpose and value.

We have as Homo sapiens the incredible privilege of exercising creative love and multiplying its influence in our world. As the Bible puts it, 'we are co-workers' with the creator (2 Corinthians 6:1).

Dr Billy Graham said at his 2005 crusade in New York at Flushing Meadows, "Today man's moral ability is lagging behind his technological ability, and it could mean disaster and catastrophe for the whole world. The greatest need in the world today is the transformation of human nature – to make us love instead of hate – and that's what we all need."[37]

The reason why there has not been a completely black picture for our world is because the love that is the light of the world does still operate as we have seen; what of course is needed is more and more individuals, us, promoting more and more love (compassion) – agape.

Love is powerful and vulnerable.It is in discovering more of this enigma and learning how to live it ,that we live out the image of our spiritual roots. To promote love, agape, compassion, is to respond to the creator. In the Christian

---

37   It is significant that this book recording Billy Graham's crusade in New York is referred to as 'possibly his last crusade' is entitled 'Living in God's Love'.

Scriptures we read, "Dear friends, let us love one another, for love comes from God. Everyone who loves has been born of God and knows God.... God is love ... no-one has ever seen God, but if we love one another, God lives in us ... (1 John 4:7,8,12) The writer of 1 John informs us that for Christians this is rooted in Jesus Christ, this love is exemplified on a cross, overcoming the ways of the world with the ways of love – proclaiming their love's answers to life's questions and proclaiming love's eternal and ultimate victory in the new life of resurrection.

In a Christian understanding God was crucifying himself in Jesus of Nazareth on a cross – love even in desolation living and victorious indicating whatever physical, mental, spiritual agonies a human may go through, the final outcome is love's eternal absolute victory.

In order for us to begin to understand this God, we need to emphasise the fact that the term 'almighty' when applied to God does not mean what the world means by almighty. It does not mean economic, military, muscle power. We have been thinking of vulnerable energy. One of the important aspects of this creative love, in the Christian tradition, called agape love is its eternal quality. In relation to Homo sapiens seen in personal terms, the continuance of personal identity and self-awareness beyond death, and in relation to the problem of suffering its vulnerability, which in fact paradoxically is its strength.

I believe it was Arthur Peacock, the theologian, who in understanding God as love in the creative process wrote "... from a recognition that God has put his own purposes at risk in creating free, self-conscious persons, we have tentatively recognised that God *suffers with* creation and in the creative process – that is, God is love …

And so our two paths to reality of science and religion begin to converge as each points to a depth of reality beyond the power of model or metaphor, in which all that is created is embraced in the inner unity of the divine life of the creator – transcendent, incarnate, and imminent. We can but echo Dante in his ultimate vision of the divine unity.

(Arthur Peacock's understanding of God's vulnerability takes the form of 'self-limitation'), "the cost of God, we may venture to say, was in a continuing self-limitation which is the negative aspect of God's creative action, and also in a self-inflicted *vulnerability* to the created processes in order to achieve an overriding purpose: the emergence of free persons. Creation is then indicated as involving for God a kind of risk, incurred lovingly and willingly and with suffering, for the greater good of a freely responsive humanity coming into existence within the created world. Love and self-sacrifice are, from this perspective, seen as inherent in the divine nature and expressed in the whole process of creation. Perhaps this is what the author of the Revelation was hinting at when he described Christ, whom he saw as now present within God as, 'The lamb slain' *from the foundation of the world.*"[38] A picture of vulnerability.

Arthur Peacock however, while recognising vulnerability in God, sees it as 'self-limitation'. What I am suggesting is somewhat different. That is seeing God as 'the Real', the

---

38   Arthur Peacock's contribution in 'The Work of Love', Creation as Kenosis, Ed John Polkinghorne, SPCK, 2001 pp.40-41

reality. So what is called 'God', 'The Real', Creator, etc. is vulnerable love, and I do not see this, in one sense as limitation, but as highlighting the nature of the kind of love we are seeing in deity. Great power is seen in great weakness – the Paradox of vulnerable love, God being God could not have acted in any other way – for then, God would not be God.

What I am suggesting is of course an attempt to understand the complications that one faces when investigating the nature of God and the universe. However, I believe this understanding of vulnerablity in creation and creator is a step in understanding God, ourselves, and the world we live in. I would agree with Arthur Peacock that when we look at the Person of Jesus of Nazareth the suggestion of vulnerability is evident, and if one accepts Jesus of Nazareth as expressing the nature of God, then one can see the suggestion of vulnerability is justified.

The power of love is seen in weakness, this is the Paradox of Love. Power to love even enemies, even in suffering – seen in the Cross of Christ, to love in ultimate vulnerability.

Arthur Peacock writes of Jesus that … his path through life was predominantly one of vulnerability to the forces that swirled around him, to which he eventually succumbed in acute suffering, and, from his human perspective, in a tragic abandoned death.

Sacrificial, self-limiting, self-giving action on behalf of others, is in human life, the hallmark of love (when responding to their spiritual roots, made in the image of God).

Because sacrificial, self-limiting, self-giving action on behalf of the good of others is, in human life, the hallmark of love, those who believe in Jesus Christ as the self-expression of God have come to see his life as their ultimate warrant for asserting that God is essentially 'love', in so far as any one word can accurately encompass God's nature. Jesus' own teaching concerning God as 'Abba' Father, and of the conditions for entering the 'kingdom of God' pointed to this too, but it was the person of Jesus and what happened to him that finally and early, established this perception of God in the Christian community."[39]

It is clear then that Jesus of Nazareth was vulnerable to the point of death. It is true that humanity reflects the creator as seen in Jesus, when people give themselves in love for others. This love can be seen however not in self-limiting, but in love going beyond limits in expanding expressions of love in life-enhancing actions.

While warming to Arthur Peacock's understanding of vulnerability, for me it does not go far enough when endeavouring to grapple with the nature of the universe, God and humanity.

This creative energy becomes personal in Jesus of Nazareth. One cannot relate meaningfully to an essence, the invisible, a 'something' that encompasses the universe yet permeates it, above, around and within. When one accepts Jesus of Nazareth as embodying in some way the author of life, yet enfolded in human form, that in seeing Jesus we see the creator, then one can begin to perceive a personal relationship with 'God', possible. And even when this person Jesus

---

39   Ibid

of Nazareth is no longer physically present, such was, is, his personality, he is still worshipped in a personal way, and God is related to in personal terms as is the Holy Spirit, because Jesus reveals God in personal terms. And known or not in personal terms, responding to love, one is still responding to a personal God.

This would bring us on to discuss the Trinity; this however is not my purpose here, and there is a host of material which is available to do this. My purpose is to highlight the concept that this Reality, God, in essence is vulnerable, and that we can have a personal relationship with this reality is evidenced by millions throughout the centuries having done so. I would suggest however that in Jesus this personal relationship becomes more intimate and the vulnerability of God made evident, especially when on the cross God is seen as suffering in the body of Jesus. The reason being, this is the length to which this kind of love will go, and is shown to be indestructible through resurrection.

It is also observable that those of whatever culture or creed who express the kind of love we are looking at are indeed relating to the God who is this love which creates. It creates understanding, forgiveness, and reconciliation. This power is seen repeatedly in vulnerable circumstances. In the epistle of John he informs us that to express this love to others is to relate to God and express the personality of God in benevolent acts, let us look at this again....

"My dear friends let us love one another, because the source of love is God. Everyone who loves is a child of God and knows God ... God has never been seen by anyone, but if we love one another, he himself dwells in us; ... this is how we know that we dwell in him and he dwells in us; he has

imparted his spirit to us ... God is love; he who dwells in love is dwelling in God, and God in him."
(1 John 4: 1.12.13.16b)

The spirit spoken of can be seen as the spirit of this love of which we speak. To acknowledge Jesus is to acknowledge this love (1 John 4: 15). To recognise Jesus' love as expressed in the vulnerability of the cross is to recognise this as the essence of love. "This is what love really is: not that we have loved God, but that he loved us and sent his son as a sacrifice to atone for our sins. If God thus loved us, my dear friends, we also ought to love one another ..."
(1 John 4: 10-11)

Jesus makes it clear that his love includes loving one's enemies; Jesus did this even in his vulnerable state on the cross. This kind of love was expressed by Mahatma Ghandi, who while never renouncing his Hindu religion, did acknowledge the love of Christ, and put this love into action even loving his enemies. This love again, as already observed, is demonstrated in circumstances of vulnerability.

This kind of love was expressed by Victor Frankl, a Holocaust survivor, an Austrian Jew, a psychologist who at thirty seven opened his own psychiatric clinic and neurology department. He was director of Rothschild Hospital in Vienna; the only hospital allowed to treat Jews. He made many false diagnoses in order to circumvent Nazi policies requiring euthanasia of the mentally ill. In 1959 he published 'Man's Search for Meaning'. He writes about the principles he developed before the war, and the application of those principles during his time as a concentration camp prisoner. He writes to heal those with a condition in which existence seems totally void of meaning. He found a piece of paper in the pocket of the clothes he wore, which belonged to a previous inmate. It read, 'Hear, O Israel, the Lord our God, the Lord is One.' In that second his perception of his personality, he said, came back.

According to Frankl, realising the meaning of life provides spiritual strength and at the moment of truth helps a person to face and cope with suffering – even the bitterest suffering. Frankl testified at the trial of an SS officer, Hoffman. Two Jewish women Holocaust survivors hid the officer after their camp was liberated and agreed to hand him over to the Americans on condition he would not be harmed. Tormented by his part in the Holocaust, Hoffman corresponded with Frankl after the war, and Frankl tried to comfort him. So again we see it is not those who appear to have the power, i.e. in this case the Nazi, but the apparent weak and vulnerable who have the power to bring life out of death by expressing love, surely the greatest power.

To recap, what I regard as crucial is this vulnerable nature of the creator, who can create in no other way. This is more than self-limiting; and when we look at the creator seen as embodied in Jesus of Nazareth, we see this carried out to the point of death which results in life even more full and rich – eternal life, this follows the logical pattern of creation as seen in what is called the 'Big Bang', a fragmentation which results in life being produced – carbon based life. But understanding humanity as both physical and spiritual, we see this logical pattern in the body of Jesus in fragmentation on the cross in the destruction of life resulting in the birth of life of a different order – 'continuity of life, but discontinuity of the old kind of life'.[40]

For the present understanding of origins, creation, and the meaning of life, we observe that love both creates and gives meaning and purpose to life; and from the perspective we have adopted cannot operate in any other way than by creating out of fragmentation and death, which is never annihilation but creation and recreation through disintegration and construction. By this, one means that out of what looks like hopelessness due to life's situations, due to the make-up of human beings and the kind of universe we live in, life again and again bursts forth, is reborn.

When we consider vulnerability as being of the very nature of that which we call – creator, God, the Real; then it may help in understanding to a limited degree the whole business of suffering in our world, when God is regarded as good and loving. So we could say that the love that created the world always and ultimately brings life out of death; and vibrant pulsating life of beautiful creativity out of all kinds of fragmentation, be it cosmic, or personal, that even the most horrific kind of death results in vibrant new life in a different sphere in a new created order.And can be tapped into in the present order as we have seen in these pages.

If we take John Polkinghorne's view that, "All of created nature is allowed to be itself according to its kind, just as human beings are allowed to be according to our kind"[41],

40 'Continuity and Discontinuity', a phrase John Polkinghorne uses – of which more later.

41 Exploring Reality, SPCK, 2005 p.143

it would follow if as human beings we are made in the image of God, then vulnerability would be part of our make-up, and the ability to remake and create; so that in dark moments of trouble, in times of break-up there can be opportunities for new beginnings no matter how dark the time may be. The darkest time many would say being death. In the Christian tradition Jesus of Nazareth has shown that even this is in fact the opportunity for life, not just a continuation of this present kind of living, but a whole new kind of life in a whole new dimension, a whole new creation, being perfected into the image of God, into that perfect love, coming back to humanity's spiritual roots, or as we have it in 1 Corinthians 13: "Now I know in part, then I shall know fully even as I am fully known", and as we have it in the letter to the Romans, chapter 8 verse 22, "We know that the whole creation has been groaning as in the pains of childbirth right up to the present time", (subjected to this, as the creator is subjected to this way of creation due to the make-up of the substance of which the creator consists) ... "Not only so, but we ourselves, who have the first fruits of the spirit, groan inwardly as we wait eagerly ... the redemption of our bodies ... the creation itself will be liberated from its bondage to decay and brought into the glorious freedom of the children of God" (Romans 8:21).

What can be seen throughout history is the power of love exercised in vulnerability. Now, some cannot believe in God because of suffering, their own, those close to them, or the worlds. But they can believe in love (compassion). And on the basis of the foundation upon which I have been building, believing in this love (compassion) though not recognised, is in fact believing in God, the Real, the creative source of all things.

The concept of God as vulnerable is a way 'through', in understanding the source of all life as a personal Deity, who can be comprehended in a universe of suffering while still accepting that which we call God as living, personal and compassionate. This in turn needs to be understood within a universe which has always produced much good and beauty in nature in things and in people.

It is of course always in a very limited degree that we understand 'God', in this world with our present understanding of life and the universe, however advanced we may consider ourselves to be, we are still going to flounder when considering the source of all life. However I believe the search for meaning to be of great importance for those who are troubled by the apparent paradox of a good loving God and the presence of suffering and evil, such as myself. For myself I have found a door of understanding opening in this exploration of vulnerability.

This work's aim as already indicated is to highlight the good. Inevitably this will mean that suffering is of necessity brought into focus, for as already made clear as pure fact there has been good of an incredible nature coming out of the darkness of suffering and in the face of much evil; even in much helplessness much hopefulness has sprung forth. This we observed has taken place in times of much violence, in times of war.

For an example of vulnerability in personal terms we turn to that wonderful book written by Philip Simmons entitled 'Learning to fall', the rewards of an imperfect life. Many people struggle with personal problems, be they health, finance, relationships, addictions, etc.; here in Philip

Simmons we have an example of how one man understood life in the face of severe handicap and vulnerability.

In 1993 Philip Simmons received the news that he had Motor Neurone Disease. He was thirty five with a wife and two young children. The usual length of life with this illness was two to five years; he lived beyond the predictions.

Rabbi Lawrence Kushner referred to Philip Simmons' book thus, - "Not only has Philip Simmons figured out the meaning of life for himself, with prodigious literary grace, he has figured out how to tell us too ..."

In his Forward to the book Philip Simmons writes, "This book is for everyone who has lived long enough to discover that life is both more and less than we hoped for." He goes on to refer to the good and bad in life; he then refers to a glimpse of something else ... "the blessings shaken out of an imperfect life like fruit from a blighted tree. We've known the dark woods, but also the moon. This book is for those ready to embrace this third way, the way through loss to a wholeness, richness, and depth we had never before envisioned."[42]

Philip Simmons in a number of ways describes how vulnerable we are as human beings. He then goes on to describe with many illustrations from life, from nature, how life can be lived at full tilt with vulnerability, as he describes it in 'Learning to Fall' ...

He writes ... "We have all suffered, and will suffer, our own falls. The fall from youthful ideals, the waning of

---

42   'Learning to Fall', Hodder, 2002

physical strength, the failure of a cherished hope, the loss of our near and dear, the fall into injury or sickness, and later or soon, the fall to our certain ends. We have no choice but to fall, and little say as to the time or the meaning. Perhaps, however, we do have some say in the manner of our falling."[43]

He speaks of mystery not as a way out but as a way in to understanding. He speaks of those moments in life when we are brought to the cliff's edge. And he writes, "At such moments we can either back away in bitterness or confusion, or leap forward into mystery. And what does mystery ask of us? Only that we be in its presence, that we fully, consciously, hand ourselves over. That is all, and that is everything.... This letting go is the first lesson of falling, and the hardest."[44]

Vulnerability is the greatest mystery when applied to God. It is a great mystery when applied to the many who while recognising the great horrors of suffering, and who themselves may very well be sufferers, still worship 'God', still love God, still pray to God, and claim a personal relationship with God; acknowledge God's interest even in the details of their personal lives, and who accept God as loving and compassionate with a purpose for their lives. Now these are facts, scientifically observable and verifiable, and need to be recognised as such. Many of those who take this view live in vulnerable circumstances, or have lived in vulnerable circumstances.

Etty Hillesum came to a strong belief in God during the

43   Ibid. pp.3-4

44   Ibid. p.8

Nazi occupation of Holland. She wrote a diary over some two and a half years. In 1942 Etty was taken to Westerbork transit camp for Dutch Jews on their way to the east. Etty would eventually be taken to Auschwitz where she died.

The last we know of her was the day she too, together with her parents and her brother Mischa, were deported on a train bound for Poland. The journey was to last three days. Before they finally left the Netherlands, Etty threw a postcard addressed to a friend out of the train. It was found and sent on by some farmers. It read, 'We left the camp singing.' They reached Auschwitz on 10th September. She died there on 30th November."[45]

Etty knew moments of weakness, of desperation, and of spiritual inspiration, she learnt through all the circumstances of her life, in the good and the bad, and in all the vulnerability of her situation. In it all she discovered God and herself, and an inner pulsating life of the spirit which would overflow and pour out to others in care, in compassion. In her vulnerability she would discover the vulnerable God. She would discover that very vulnerability was the very facet which would develop her belief in the reality of God in her belief in love and rejection of hate.

"The conviction deepened in her that at the root of the human heart lie goodness and love. Not, despite all the evidence, malice and evil. And so she remains determined that she will refuse hatred ..."

---

45 Etty Hillesum, A Life Transformed, Patrick Woodhouse, Continuum, 2009 p.3. Reproduced by kind permission of Continuum International Publishing Group. Reproduced by kind permission of Continuum International Publishing Group.

As one reads her, one is reminded of the words of Dietrich Bonhoeffer writing to his friend Eberhard Bethge from his prison cell in Flossenburg just nine months before he is hanged by the Nazis. 'God allows himself to be edged out of the world and on to the cross', and so is 'weak and powerless'. But Bonhoeffer insists 'that is exactly the way, the only way in which he can be with us and help us.' Etty arrives at the same insight.[46]

She knows about all the cruelty and sadism, ... "I know it all ... and yet – at unguarded moments, when left to myself, I suddenly lie against the naked breast of life, and her arms round me are so gentle and so protective, and my own heartbeat is difficult to describe, so slow and regular and so soft, almost muffled, but so constant, as if it would never stop, and so good and merciful as well. That is also my attitude to life, and I believe that neither war nor any other senseless human atrocity will ever be able to change it." ...

She writes that "it is good to live even behind barbed wire and draughty barracks if one lives with the necessary love for people and for life."[47]

Love is very vulnerable and very powerful; the image of the creator was in Etty and worked out through her in her developing attitudes. The attitude developed is patterned on the vulnerable Jesus on the cross, refusing to hate but rather giving out love to all, enemies included, and in that love giving life eternal, for love is eternal.

---

46   Ibid p.45f

47   Ibid. pp.49-50, 150-151

The paradox of God is that the weak powerless God is the power of God, because God's power is expressed in vulnerability.

Paul Tillich, who developed his teaching career as a theologian and philosopher in Germany where he was born and grew up, was deeply aware of what the Holocaust meant. He wrote of the triumph of love, so evident in Etty in all the vulnerability of her life, in one of his published sermons two years before his death.

'It is love human and divine, which overcomes death in nation and generations and in all the horror of our time … Death is given power over everything finite, especially in our period of history. But death is given no power over love. Love is stronger. It creates something new out of the destruction caused by death; it bears everything and overcomes everything. It is at work where the power of death is strongest, in war and persecution and homelessness and hunger and physical death itself. It is omnipresent, and here and there in the smallest and most hidden ways as in the greatest and most visible ones, it rescues life from death. It reaches each of us, for love is stronger than death' …[48]

On 13th October 1942 Etty Hillesum wrote the final sentence of the diary which has survived her. It reads:

'We should be willing to act as a balm for all wounds.'"[49]

We can conclude that love is powerful in weakness. That

---

48   Ibid. pp.152-153

49   Ibid. pp.152-153

it works again and again in vulnerable circumstances. It is seen in the concentration camps; it is seen in the vulnerability brought on by illness; It is seen in hope coming from despair, and bringing a kind of balm in the complexities of suffering and disability.

I think of a lady, who was once a ballerina teacher who then became ill with M.S., no longer able to walk or use her arms, hands, with hardly any speech, in a vulnerable condition, depending on others for even the intimate administration of hygiene, etc. Yet a lady who lives in the knowledge of Jesus as Saviour, in the knowledge of the love of God, who attends regular worship and expresses her faith even within the limitations and vulnerability of her situation. We thank God for her words. We thank God that words can be so precious, and we thank God that compassion is also expressed when we can't find words.

There is a story told by Philip Yancey that speaks of the help one can bring to another in vulnerability by sharing vulnerability.

Betsy Burnham in a book written shortly before her death from Cancer told about one of the most meaningful letters she received during her illness:

'Dear Betsy,
I am afraid and embarrassed. With the problems you are facing, what right do I have to tell you I am afraid? I have found one excuse after another for not coming to see you. With all my heart, I want to reach out and help you and your family. I want to be available and useful. Most of all, I want to say the words

that will make you well. But the fact remains
that I am afraid. I have never before written
anything like this. I hope you will understand
and forgive me.

Love, Anne.'

Anne could not find the personal strength needed to make
herself available to her friend, but at least she shared her
honest feelings with Betsy and made herself vulnerable.
That to was a form of availability.

Another woman, reflecting on letters that she and her
husband received in the midst of a family tragedy, told me
that the letters' very clumsiness made them meaningful to
her. Many writers would apologise for their ineptness not
knowing what to say. But to her the anguished groping
for words was the whole point: their 'sheer floundering
confusion' best expressed what she and her family were
feeling too."[50]

These are examples of people feeling their vulnerability,
weakness, inability, both those who are suffering and those
seeking to offer help.

Jesus Christ on the cross was of course in a most horrifi-
cally vulnerable position. Yet his great weakness became
the occasion of great strength; the power of almighty love,
the kind that overcomes hate, will not return hate for hate,
and offers forgiveness. From great weakness came forth
great strength. It needs great strength to love one's enemies
in that way. Even though he experienced feeling terribly

---

50 Philip Yancey – Were is God When it Hurts,Zondervan
1997,p.p.183-184.

isolated, deserted by God and man, with his last gasping breaths offers forgiveness, that is the power of heartfelt love in the midst of vulnerability.

Now if in some way this Jesus of Nazareth is also God, or embodying the very spirit of God (of love, agape) evidenced by the power of love in vulnerability, it points to the vulnerability of 'God', the 'Real', source of creation. We could go on to assert on this basis that love in vulnerability is the world's salvation.

It is of significance that the record of the first Christian martyr after Jesus of Nazareth, Stephen, also cries out not to have this sin laid upon his executioners. (Acts 7:59) "While they were stoning him, Stephen prayed, 'Lord Jesus, receive my spirit', then he fell on his knees and cried out, 'Lord, do not hold this sin against them.'"

"The late Canon W.H. Vanstone has written (in the Progress of Love) each step is a precarious step into the unknown, in which each triumph contains new potential for tragedy, and each tragedy can be redeemed into a wider triumph."

In understanding the Bible this is surely to be seen as that through which we interpret the scriptures. If we understand love as exemplified in Jesus demonstrating its power in apparent weakness on the cross, as *the* power, then the understanding of a destructive God, having the same kind of power that human despots have, muscle power, then we paradoxically weaken the 'power' of God, whose real strength as we have seen lies in a different kind of power, the kind Jesus of Nazareth exemplified on the cross. This was not the kind of power seen in a God who wreaks havoc on his enemies.

"It is the person of Christ, to whom the Bible witnesses. This means that any interpretation of a Biblical text that fails to see it in the light of God's will to redeem all humanity, to go to any lengths to do so, and finally to accomplish what God intends, fails to get the message of the Bible. It is because of this that an interpretation which depicts God as vengeful, vindictive, exclusive to just a few chosen people, or purely retributive, falls short of the Christian insight that 'God is love' (1 John 4:16), and that God's love knows no limits (neither height nor depth, nor anything else in all creation, will be able to separate us from the love of God that is in Christ Jesus our Lord.' Romans 8:39) The Bible gives us its own main principle of interpretation when it tells us that the love of God in Jesus is the culminating point of its teaching. Only when we keep that firmly in mind can we be sure of being true to what the Bible really teaches."[51] And this is how we view words attributed to Jesus if they do not express his forgiveness and compassion, how can they be of him?

Of course trying to understand the complexity of a love so powerful because it is so vulnerable is bound at some point to go beyond what can be explained in rational terms. When Jesus is recorded saying, 'love your enemies' seen in all its starkness appears unreasonable, irrational, but for all that, it is the answer to a world that has constantly sought to solve its problems through violence in words and actions.

---

51 What the Bible Really Says, SPCK, 2004 p.27

And we thank God that there have been those who have actually put the words of Jesus into practice, and have by their actions shown love toward their enemies.

Although there is the problem of evil and suffering in our world, the fact remains, even though we have not worked it all out, (been able to answer all the 'why' questions) there is an undeniable silver lining in life which is active and always has been in the expressions of compassionate love in an uncountable number of people in all kinds of vulnerable circumstances.

Cosmologists predict the ultimate demise of the universe due to expansion or collapse. If expansion wins the day, the universe will get increasingly colder and dilate, if gravity wins through, what as Polkinghorne puts it, "began with a big bang, will end in a big crunch as the universe implodes into a cosmic melting pot."[52]

This however would simply be further evidence of a cycle of death, creation and recreation being the very stuff of which we and the universe are made. Accepting the Big Bang theory, that out of death comes life, the birth of the universe, you and me, from the remains of dead stars; carbon based life. Again we have those words of John Polkinghorne, "Although the universe appears to have been lifeless for the first eleven billion years of its existence, there is a real sense in which it was pregnant with the possibility of life from the very beginning."[53]

As I see it the foundational principle of life, be it in personal

---

52   The God of Hope and the End of the World,.p.9.

53   Polkinghorne, Ibid,.p.p.4-5

or cosmic terms is life out of death, death is never what it seems, life is produced out of what we call death, hope is always positively ultimately realised. Hence whenever and however this universe ends, again out of death will come new life.

It is I feel necessary to say that if vulnerability is the very essence of creation and creator, and this can certainly be seen in creation, in humanity and in the universe at large, then it cannot be emphasised enough to say that almighty love is almighty vulnerability and creativity. And it is in vulnerability that compassion is evident. From what we have so far endeavoured to unravel, while this leaves, as noted, big questions yet to be answered, it does most positively state in very essence that the very worst vulnerable position one feels oneself to be in, does not have the last word, and even if one were to be unable to grasp the truth of compassion and operate its power in vulnerability, the vulnerable love that is the source of all creation and recreation, being the ultimate vulnerability, will see one through to ultimate life. Death, which one could say is the ultimate evidence of individual vulnerability, is no barrier to the creative energy that actually of its very nature brings life again and again out of death, this can be seen as much a truth of the individual as of the cosmos.

The whole of creation is subject to vulnerability, yet out of that very circumstance, life is again and again brought forth, so that even in what one can consider the greatest vulnerability, life is produced; the universe itself will be made new from its vulnerable essence. (Romans 8:18-25)

From our Christian perspective I come back again and again to the record of Jesus of Nazareth's crucifixion. Even though 'feeling' forsaken by God the Father, and by all, out of that desolation came life. It is important in personal terms to recognise 'feelings' did not have the last word on the cross; one could say, never were feelings farther from fact; the human understanding, the emotional and physical vulnerability of the cross, was we say pregnant with life; out of this death came pulsating life, life for the universe, for love could not be destroyed on that cross, compassion was poured forth, even from such a place, in such darkness came such light as has never been put out in life or in death, and life was to use a phrase 'born again', from all creation.

This goes beyond knowledge; our knowledge is limited. Love has depths and a vastness which will always stretch us beyond the boundaries of present understanding, and enables life to be lived in the present though not confined by the present, to be explored and embraced even when knowledge reaches its boundaries. The love that we are exploring continues to embrace us beyond the temporal to the eternal. We shall look at the limitations of knowledge in our next chapter.

Paul places his assurance in this love that the vulnerable Jesus poured out from that cross.

"No, in all these things we have complete victory through him who loved us! For I am certain that nothing can separate us from his love: neither death nor life, neither angels nor other heavenly rulers or powers, neither the present nor the future, neither the world above nor the world below – there is nothing in all creation that will ever be able to separate us from the love of God which is ours through Christ Jesus our Lord."

(Romans 8:37-39 GNB)

Martin Buber had it right when he said, "If you wish to believe, love." For him the meaning of life is to penetrate it with love. This vulnerable love goes beyond the comprehension available to human intellect.

Chapter 3.

Love and limitations of knowledge

Ruth Gledhill, religious correspondent for the Times Newspaper, had an interview with Richard Dawkins, the well-known biologist and critic of religion; she observes that his passion and anger stem from a love for truth. In the interview Richard Dawkins states,

"I am a scientist, it is my business to understand and help others understand the nature of life in my case, or generally, as a scientist, the nature of the universe. At the beginning of the 21st century, humanity is approaching a staggeringly impressively near-to-complete understanding. It's hugely exciting to be a member of this elite species at this time when our understanding of physics, biology, and cosmology is so exciting and near complete."[54]

One cannot help observing, if this reportage is correct, that this commendable love and search for truth by an eminent biologist has led him, sadly, to a very narrow view of reality. We are indeed most grateful and indebted to scientists for much of the wonderful work they have done

---

54   The Times, Thursday 10th May 2007

and are doing in discovering more and more about the universe. However, it is surely not true to say we are near-to-complete understanding. This kind of thinking falls into the trap of those who felt genetics to be the full and final answer to what life is all about! This leaves a whole range of human experience untouched. The universe is surely so vast, how can we have a near-to-complete knowledge of it? Homo sapiens knowledge will always be limited to a lesser or greater degree, and when endeavouring to comprehend the divine will always flounder at some point. We even find difficulty in unravelling the immensity of the universe, let alone the source, the creator.

"There are over 100 million galaxies in the universe that we can observe from our planet earth, and our galaxy 'The Milky Way' is just one of them. There are over 100 million stars in a typical galaxy, and our star, the sun, is just one of them. We have been able to see galaxies about ten thousand million light years away, and we are still moving apart at about three-fifths of the speed of light. Light travels at 186,000 miles per second. It travels from the sun to earth – a distance of 93 million miles – in about eight minutes Light takes ten thousand million years to travel from some of the farthest galaxies we can see."[55]

To come to the point where one could say we have a near-to-complete understanding would require an exploration of every 'nook and cranny' of even our own galaxy, let alone the millions we can and can't see.

Fellow atheist and scientist Peter Atkins makes claims

---

[55]   Keith Ward, 'Christianity, a Guide for the Perplexed', SPCK, 2007 p.1

similar to Richard Dawkins; Keith Ward, one time Regius Professor of Divinity, Oxford University, quotes him as saying, "there is nothing that cannot be understood' (in his book Creation Revisited). Keith Ward observes, "This is a remarkably bold statement of faith. It goes well beyond all available evidence, since at present there are millions of things we do not understand including the fundamentals of quantum physics."[56]

It is also a fact that what at one time is regarded by science as 'fact' may well have to be revised in the light of new knowledge. Dr Martyn Lloyd Jones, one time Chief Clinical Assistant to Sir Thomas Horder, the King's Physician has written …

"If you study the history of science you will have much less respect for its supposed supreme authority than you had when you began. It is nothing but a simple fact of history to say that a hundred years ago and less, scientists were teaching dogmatically and with extreme confidence that the thyroid gland, the pituitary gland and other glands were nothing but vestigial remains. They said that they had no value and no function whatsoever. Now this is not theory. It is fact. They asserted dogmatically that these were useless remains. But today we know that these glands are essential to life. Without arguing in details about scientific matters … it is ignorant to accord to 'science', 'modern knowledge' or 'learning' an authority which they really do not possess. Let us be scientifically sceptical with regard to the assertions of 'science'. Let us remember that so many of their assertions are mere suppositions and

---

56   Source not found

theories which cannot be proved, and which may very well be disproved, as so many have been disproved during the past hundred years."[57]

We of course benefit enormously from science, but it is not, as the facts bear out, a 'supreme' authority. And just as there are 'facts' yet to be unravelled by science and wonders still to be discovered which at the present time are still a puzzle, so it is with the spiritual dimension to life.

As regards coming to an understanding of what we call 'God' or the 'Real' as John Hick refers to the Deity, ultimate knowledge is beyond us in this life whether it be in science or religion, or spirituality. It calls for a humble recognition of this by all, while at the same time seeking to discover as much as we are able. This can be an exciting journey of research and discovery as more and more is revealed in both science and religion.

But it is not only through the intellect that one comes to know God. There are other avenues by which people have come to know God.

It is reported that Helen Keller, blind, deaf and dumb as a child, had learnt through her teacher to communicate through touch. On one occasion her teacher, Anne Sullivan with her finger spelt out on Helen's hand the letters, G.O.D. Helen communicated back through touch, "I know him, but I have never known his name."

Martyn Lloyd Jones quoting Blaise Pascal, the great French mathematician and scientist writes, "The supreme achieve-

---

57 'Authority', The Banner of Truth Trust, 1958 reprint 1985, p.40

ment of reason is to bring us to see that there is a limit to reason", and Martyn Lloyd Jones comments, "There it seems to me is the starting point. Use your reason, use your intellect; do so honestly, and you will come to the conclusion that there is a limit to reason."[58]

Antony Flew, the well-known atheist, came to a theistic view of the universe in 2004. In 2000 he is reported to have said he will go wherever the evidence leads him, this is to be applauded. We admire and respect Antony Flew's frankness and honesty.

However, it has to be noted that just because one does not have evidence for whatever the object of research is, does not mean there is no evidence, evidence could well be there all the time waiting to be discovered. There will always be a limit to reason; even the greatest brain will come to that point.

Just because one lacks the means to measure, does not mean what cannot be measured does not exist, this is self-evident. It simply points to a limitation of present knowledge. Just because our present level of experience and understanding does not allow us, as far as verifiable facts are concerned, to produce to our satisfaction, 'proof', is no evidence that something does not exist,for example, just because we have no understanding of a life that does not end,ie goes on beyond death, is no ground for saying it does end. Just because all we know about time spans, longevity, is that it has a beginning and an end does not cancel out an eternal dimension, after all is there an end to

---

58   Ibid. p.13

time, to the universe? And what do we mean when some talk of 'out of time'?

Simply to disbelieve because we are faced with something beyond our comprehension is no good scientific ground for saying it is not possible. The microscopic world has been around for a very long time, long before the first microscope was invented in 1609.[59] Just because it could not be seen before this date does not mean it did not exist before this date! At so many levels there is so much yet to be discovered, macro and micro worlds, the human body, the mind, the natural world, etc. It is surely unscientific to say we have reached a 'near- complete- understanding', Surely we should be prepared to see beyond the wonders we know to the wonders we don't know.

Jacquetta Hawkes, the wife of the late J.B. Priestly wrote ... "In all this realm of ultimate meaning there is only one thing I believe with certainty - that we live in an impenetrable mystery. The more that we find out about the universe, the greater this mystery becomes. Our discoveries inspire us with unending wonder, but not with final understanding."[60]

Malcolm Muggeridge would want to go beyond what science can reveal in order to understand life ... "as far as I am concerned, is there any recompense in the so-called achievements of science. It is true that in my lifetime more progress has been made in unravelling the composition and

---

59   Invented by the Dutch spectacle maker, Zacharias Jenssen, 1580-1638

60   From 'What I Believe', Allen & Unwin, 1966, Ed by George Unwin, p.137

mechanism of the material universe than previously in the whole of recorded time. This does not at all excite my mind, or even my curiosity. The atom has been split; the universe has been discovered, and will soon be explored. Neither achievement has any bearing on what alone interests me – which is why life exists, and what is the significance, if any, of my minute and so transitory part in it.

Why, then, should going to the moon and Mars, or spending a holiday along the Milky Way, be expected to advance me further in my quest than going to Manchester and Liverpool, or spending a holiday in Brighton? Education, the great mumbo-jumbo and fraud of the age, purports to equip us to live, and is prescribed as a universal remedy for everything from juvenile delinquency to premature senility. For the most part, it only serves to enlarge stupidity, inflate conceit, enhance credulity, and put those subjected to it at the mercy of brain-washers with printing presses, radio and television at their disposal ..."[61]

While we may not be so scathing and unappreciative of science and education as Malcolm Muggeridge, there is truth in his exaggerations, as the meaning of life lies well beyond what science, with all its wonderful achievements, can reveal.

J.B. Priestly commenting on understanding life quotes Jung, "As far as I can see – and I claim no prophetic insight – that task is to bring consciousness to the life of the earth, or, as Jung wrote in his old age, 'to kindle a light in the darkness of mere being.' We cannot perform this service, just as we cannot even enjoy a good life, unless our minds

---

61   Ibid. pp.139-140

and personalities are free to develop in their own fashion, outside the iron moulds of totalitarian states and systems, narrow and authoritarian churches, and equally narrow and dogmatic scientific – positive opinion ...

I think the last is just as dangerous as the other two. Great scientists, creative men, are imaginative and open-minded, but the men below them together with the scientific workers and technologists, whose numbers are rapidly increasing, too often think and behave as if science were a dogmatic religion. It is they who shout 'mere coincidental!' when any example of precognition or extra-sensory perception is offered them. They dismiss anything that cannot be tested in the lab. And the danger here is that just when we might acquire new and valuable knowledge about ourselves, we may be brought to a halt by a sheer weight of prejudice. Had this attitude of mind always prevailed, there would have been no science at all."[62]

Sadly it is not only scientific workers and technologists (and of course not all of them) but even some at the 'top' who behave as if science were a dogmatic religion! What we have been researching here has been tested in the 'lab of life', and has been found to work again and again, been found to be 'real', life-giving, and enhancing.

A distinguished scientist once said, not himself a religious believer, "Science cannot answer questions philosophers or children ask: why are we here, what is the point of being alive, how ought we to behave? Genetics has almost nothing to say about what makes people more than just mechanics driven by biology, about what makes us human ... in its

---

62   Ibid. pp.164-165

early days human genetics suffered greatly from its high opinions of itself. It failed to understand its limits."[63]

Of course, we might like to ask the question, is there certain knowledge on any subject available to us? Bertrand Russell puts it like this –

"Is there any knowledge in the world which is so certain that no reasonable man would doubt it? This question, which at first sight might not seem difficult, is really one of the most difficult that can be asked. When we have realised the obstacles in the way of a straightforward and confident answer, we shall be well launched on the study of philosophy – for philosophy is merely the attempt to answer such ultimate questions, not carelessly and dogmatically, as we do in ordinary life and even in the sciences, but critically after exploring all that makes such questions puzzling, and after realising all the vagueness and confusion that underlie our ordinary ideas."[64]

I maintain there is indeed a knowledge which no reasonable person would doubt, and we are here exploring the truth of such a statement. The knowledge I am referring to is that which Bertrand Russell longed for, compassion, or to put it another way, Christian love, as he phrased it. (See Chapter one, page one)

This love is absolute not in the sense that we know all about it, but in the sense that there is no doubt it is the answer to the meaning of our lives; at least a meaning which is

---

63   Quoted by Richard Harries in 'God Outside the Box', SPCK, p.60, from Professor Steve Jones

64   The Case for Christianity, Lion, 1981, Colin Chapman, p.20

paramount whatever any other reasons there may be. It is the answer to the questions, Why are we here? What is the point of being alive? How ought we to behave? We are seeking to understand that kind of love that does indeed 'kindle a light in the darkness of mere being' as Jung puts it. It is this love that kindles this light, and places value on life.

This love sets one's mind free to develop beyond the restrictive moulds of narrow-minded prejudices, but which does lead to the assertion that this is the answer to the meaning and purpose of our lives. What we cannot be dogmatic about is how this will operate in each person's life and in every situation, and that we shall never in this life plumb the depths of such a concept, but there is a joy and anticipation in the exploration of it, and exploring this love means living it as our understanding of it develops.

Paul writing in a Christian context expresses this love in a prayer for the Christian church: "And I pray that you being rooted and established in love (agape) may have power, together with all the saints, to grasp how wide and long and high and deep is the love of Christ, and to know this love that surpasses knowledge – that you may be filled to the measure of all the fullness of God." (Ephesians 3: 17-19)

However, I see this love as not exclusive to Christianity, as a Christian I would root it in, as already noted, the cross of Christ, but of course it is to be seen operating in many different religions, and those of no particular religion.

Thich Nhat Hanh, a Buddhist monk, has said, "True seeing always gives rise to true love."[65]

John Humphrys, a self-confessed agnostic, to whom I have already referred, is an agnostic who is very open and fair minded, at least that's how he comes over to me in his book. He believes there is more to life than our genetic biological makeup. He writes,

" … We are more than the sum of our genes – selfish or otherwise – but you might not think so if you read only the works and listened only to the words of the atheist evolutionists. They have precious little to say about our 'fundamental awareness of the difference between good and evil'. Nor do they have much to say about love.

On the shelves in my office are rows of books about belief written by some great biologists, physicists, philosophers, sceptics and theologians of our time. Millions of words, a great store of knowledge and sometimes, wisdom. But there is nothing that gets to the heart of it with the power and the beauty of these few verses from a book many of those writers affect to despise." The end of that beautiful passage ends with these words -

What we see now is like a dim image in a mirror; then we shall see face to face. What I know now is only partial; then it will be complete – as complete as God's knowledge of me.

65   Thich Nhat Hanh, Essential Writings, Ed by Robert Ellesberg, Orbis Books, 2001, p.105. Reprinted from The Teachings on Love(1998) by Thich Nhat Hanh with permission of Parallax Press ,Berkeley,California,www.Parallax.org Reprinted from The Teachings on Love(1998) by Thich Nhat Hanh with permission of Parallax Press ,Berkeley,California,www.Parallax.org

Meanwhile these three remain: faith, hope and love; and the greatest of these is love.
(1 Corinthians 13)

"That's it, isn't it? Has there ever been a greater description of love? For St Paul of all people to pronounce that love is a greater virtue even than faith says a great deal. He could scarcely be clearer on the subject. When everything else is stripped away, it is love that remains. It is what makes us what we are. It distinguishes us from every other living creature."[66]

As John Humphreys observes, knowledge is limited in what it can convey about humanity, even faith is limited to a subordinate position, for love is the greatest. This love is seen in action in the lives of all kinds of people in all kinds of circumstances as we have noted.

Humphry observes this love is expressed in the life of all who have....

"... acted out of pure selflessness at risk to themselves to save others. Christians would say the supreme example was Jesus. We cannot describe their actions in Darwinian terms."[67]

This love is manifest whenever it is expressed in caring compassion and understanding, it will not always involve risk of life, but it will always seek the best for others welfare.

---

66   'In God we Doubt, Confessions of a Failed Atheist', Hodder & Stoughton, 2007, p.280-283

67   Ibid

It is a fact clearly evident throughout history that acts of compassion are as much a part of history as acts of violence. 'The transcendental experience at the heart of human nature', has been and is demonstrated constantly, without this facet in the life of humanity the world would be a dark place indeed. We are reminded again of the words in John's gospel chapter one:

"The light shines in the darkness, and the darkness has never put it out." John 1:5 (GNB)

It is possible to take the view that some of our questions just cannot be answered solely by science; that an understanding of spirituality for example would enable us to go further in understanding ourselves and our universe.

Keith Ward draws our attention to –

Clifford Geortz who gives an understanding appraisal of religious beliefs as being important in our evaluation of humanity; this includes the spiritual. Religion, he says, affirms that reality is ultimately explicable, that suffering is endurable, and that there is a moral order to reality …

… If it explains the inexplicable, makes suffering bearable, and refers to a moral order that is not open to empirical investigation, it must posit an underlying reality. The religious perspective Geortz says, 'moves beyond the realities of everyday life to wider ones, which are experienced in ritual activity, points at which we worship – commit ourselves to – something that is not ourselves. Darwin's theory of natural selection just will not fill the bill. If taken as a total explanation, it eliminates the credibility of worship, and denies that there is any order to reality."[68]

That people want to know the answers to questions with regard to ourselves, our world, our universe, is of course undeniable, of all the animal kingdom Homo sapiens want to know 'why?' and 'where are we going?'

Tennessee Williams, the American dramatist, wrote, "What are we sure of? Not even of our existence, dear comforting friend! And whom can we ask the questions that torment us? What is this place? Where are we? A fat old man who gives sly hints that only bewilder us more, a fake of a gipsy squinting at cards and tea leaves. What else are we offered? The never broken procession of little events that assure us that we and strangers about us are still going on? Where? Why? And the perch that we hold is unstable! We're threatened with eviction, for this is a port of entry and departure, there are no permanent quests! And where else have we to go when we leave? … We're lonely. We're frightened."[69]

Of course not everyone is tormented by these questions, they just don't think too much about them, or when they do, it's in some milder way or more intensely when some dramatic event occurs in their lives, or in the life of the world. In their moments of reflection I would suggest most people identify with some aspects of Tennessee Williams'

---

68 'Religion as a Cultural System' in the Interpretation of Cultures, New York, Basic Books, 1973, p.90, quoted by Keith Ward in 'The Case for Religion'

69 Quoted in 'The Case for Christianity', Colin Chapman, Lion, p.10

thoughts. Without some understanding of our purpose in life, we are left with this very negative response of Williams, whereas with a reason and a foundation we can begin to build.

With all our great knowledge, with all the commendable intellectual pursuit for meaning, we realise that intellectual achievements and researches do not offer all that humans want in life, do not answer all our questions. The philosopher Friedrich Nietzsche (1844-1900) used all his intellectual powers to build his life on the assumption that God was dead. He ended his life in trying to live with a philosophy of nihilism, he endeavoured to live his philosophy of meaninglessness to the end which in his case led him to ultimate madness.

In order to live a meaningful life, some kind of foundation is a help, some would say essential, and for some this is God. Sir Christopher Frayling, a professor of cultural history an historian, broadcaster and journalist, as a postgraduate studying for his PhD, he was surrounded by astro-physicians, biologists, physicists, who thought they were squeezing out God or any need for God. He writes,

"Actually, there were some jolly big questions. Even today, when I hear Richard Dawkins talking about it – and he's very extreme – it upsets me. The arrogance. It's bad science, bad philosophy, to be so shrill: 'We don't need God, we don't need cheap supernatural explanations', as he puts it.

In the late 1960's, too, I remember people were saying the same thing. I keep saying, 'yes, but actually you can analyse the big bangs, you can look at the origin of the universe, you can look at evolution, but all it does is put the questions about God into a deeper place than it was before i.e. why have all the elements ended up in the way that they have? That's not a question that scientists ask."[70]

"The claim that science is the only way to truth is a claim ultimately unworthy of science itself. Nobel Laureate Sir Peter Madawar points this out in his excellent book 'Advice to a Young Scientist': There is no quicker way for a scientist to bring discredit upon himself and upon his profession than roundly to declare particularly when no declaration of any kind is called for, that science knows, or soon will know, the answers to all questions worth asking, and that questions which do not admit a scientific answer are in some way non-questions or, 'pseudo-questions' that only simpletons ask and only the gullible profess to be able to answer. Madawar goes on to say, 'the existence of a limit to science is, however, made clear by its inability to answer childlike elementary questions having to do with first and last things – questions such as, 'How did everything begin?' 'What are we all here for?' 'What is the point of living?' …

Francis Collins, Director of the Human Genome Project, also emphasises this: 'Science is powerless to answer questions such as 'why did the universe come into being?' 'What is the meaning of human existence?' 'What happens after we die?' There is clearly no inconsistency involved in being a passionately committed scientist at the highest level while simultaneously recognising that science cannot

---

70   'Devout Sceptics', Ed Bel Mooney, Hodder, p.61

answer every kind of question, including some of the deepest questions that human beings can ask."[71]

Jean-Paul Sartre, the French philosopher (1905-80) came to the point where he believed there is no purpose to existence, only nothingness. It is extremely sad that thinkers such as Sartre, Nietzsche, and in our own day scientists such as Peter Atkins and Richard Dawkins, have no answers for the really big questions of life, and only offer a bleak kind of meaningless philosophy as regards ultimate human destiny; what is even sadder, they make dogmatic statements through tunnel vision which refuses to research the most crucial areas with regard to ultimate questions. Some, such as Richard Dawkins, even stoop to ridicule those with a different view. In my view however the only salvation for them and all of us is the compassion (love) which is found at the very centre of life and, as has been noted again and again, operates constantly and consistently in spite of all the wrongs that encompass it, and which ultimately moves beyond the temporal to the eternal.

That well known broadcaster and journalist, the agnostic John Humphrys has commented "Sartre's conclusion is too bleak for me. Trite it may be, but most of us can see the beauty as well as the horrors of the world, and sometimes humanity at its most noble. We sense a spiritual element in the nobility and in the miracle of unselfish love and sacrifice, something beyond our conscious understanding. You don't need to be an eastern mystic or a devout religious believer to feel that. We should not – we must not – be brow-beaten by arrogant atheists, and meekly accept their

---

71   'God's Undertaker', John Lennox, Lion, 2007 p.41

deluded label. They are no more capable of understanding this most profound mystery than a small child making his first awe-inspiring discoveries."[72]

Bertrand Russell, though believing all definite knowledge is from science is honest and realistic enough to admit that "most of the interesting questions lie outside its competence ..., is the world divided into mind and matter, and if so, what is mind, what is matter? Is mind subject to matter, or is it possessed of independent powers? Has the universe any unity or purpose? Is it evolving towards some goal? Are there really laws of nature, or do we believe in them only because of our innate love of order? Is man what he seems to the astronomer, a tiny lump of impure carbon and water impotently crawling on a small and unimportant planet? Or is he what he appears to Hamlet? Is there a way of living that is noble and another that is base, or are all ways of living merely futile? ... To such questions no answers can be found in the laboratory."[73]Is there something, someone, behind all this order? This work states there is.

So some knowledge is outside the scope of the laboratory, says Russell. His questions come down to questions of meaning and purpose. So we can say something is going on 'outside the laboratory'. Simply because one cannot understand all that is 'going on' in whatever context, does not mean something very real is not going on. The title of this chapter indicates there are limitations of knowledge. There

---

72   John Humphrys 'In God We Doubt', Hodder, 2007, pp.321-322 (Confessions of a Failed Atheist)

73   Source not found

is 'mystery' because we do not have a brain big enough to grasp all that is going on.

Alister McGrath in response to Richard Dawkins comment "that religious people who talk about 'mystery' are just irrational mystics who are too lazy or frightened to use their minds properly" makes the following observation:

"It is a recognisable caricature of the idea of 'mystery'. But it's still a caricature. Here's what a theologian means when using the word 'mystery', something which is true and possesses its own rationality, yet which the human mind finds it impossible to grasp fully. Some years ago, I started learning Japanese. I didn't get very far. The language uses two syllabaries, has a vocabulary which bears little relation to any of the languages that I knew, and a syntax that seemed completely illogical to my western way of thinking. In short, I couldn't make sense of it. But my failure to grasp the Japanese language represents a failure on my part. Those who know the language assure me that it is rational and intelligible; it's just that I can't get my mind around it ...

'Mystery' McGrath goes on to explain ... "may lie beyond the present capacity of human reason to grasp; that does not mean it is contrary to reason, as Thomas Aquinas emphasised. The human mind is just too limited to grasp the totality of such a reality and we must therefore do what we can while recognising our limits."[74]

"Man's knowledge is incomplete. It is not that his science is unimportant, indeed it is the most essential tool he has. But

---

74   'Dawkins God', Blackwell Publishing, 2005 p.154

he must remember that it is limited; to forget those limits is dangerous. Science will never quite explain his personal existence or the far flung universe beyond his grasp. His search for the point of life must continue; but perhaps the search itself is sufficient meaning for his existence."[75]But I maintain it is crucial we explore from a foundation of Love,Agape,the ultimate reason for living.

So there are mysteries acknowledge by scientists. And there are mysteries that cannot be unravelled in a laboratory. What I maintain gives meaning is compassionate love; to continue to reach out for this and apply it is the most important research in this or any other universe. Bertrand Russell recognised the one thing that is needed, is love.[76]This he informs us was one of the great passions of his life,for this to be activated.This he saw as the answer to the 'destructive evil passions in human minds.

With all the knowledge, all the intellectual power that could ever be obtained, without this love there is no meaning to life. Without this compassion, hatred and bitterness would go unchecked, and there would be no way out of the meaningless philosophies of revenge, nothing to cut the cycle of hate and misunderstanding. With this love, there is hope for the present and for the future. There is life to be lived, good life, and there is an understanding of life, that has a big vision, so big that it sees life lived on such a scale that it embraces eternity as well. In this acceptance, we are accepting mystery, we could say the greatest mystery of all, eternal life, resurrection. It is to this mystery that we now turn our attention.

---

75   Albert Winston, 'The Story of God', Bantam Press, p.336

76   Chapter one, page one of this book

Chapter 4.

Love through Crucifixion and Resurrection

Mysteries are to be found in every walk of life, in science, art, religion, and macro and micro worlds. There are those who while accepting there are mysteries in life, find it difficult to accept mystery in religion. It is however just as true in religion as elsewhere; there are aspects of life that simply go beyond the capacity of present available knowledge.

Some have real problems in accepting a bodily resurrection of Jesus of Nazareth. Richard Holloway, is such, a man of compassion who has sought to open a door of understanding for those who have an intellectual barrier regarding the resurrection of Jesus. He endeavours therefore to divest the resurrection of Jesus of what we call the miraculous, which as already observed is that which is beyond our present ability to work out, a point it's important to emphasise.

Richard Holloway writes, "Resurrection is the refusal to be imprisoned any longer by history and its long hatreds; it is the determination to take the first step out of the tomb. It may be a personal circumstance that immobilises us, or a social evil that confronts us. Whatever it is, we simply refuse any longer to accept it because the logic of resurrection calls us to action. More importantly it means joining with others in action to bring new life to human communities that are still held in the grip of death."[77]

Now while this is a genuine attempt to help those with intellectual problems, there are many that find this kind of explanation impossible to accept. The overcoming of hatreds, etc. is of course very commendable, but all this is possible without recourse to resurrection of any kind. Many religions and those with no religion at all recognise the crucial importance of overcoming hatreds, etc. And we would all surely wish to work together to bring life to communities that are held in the grip of death; all those committed to peace and reconciliation would wish this. Resurrection means all things will ultimately be put right, an answer will be given to the mix of right and wrong.

This bypassing of the natural way of understanding 'resurrection' i.e. bodily resurrection (a person dead, brought to life again) has nothing to say regarding those who find little meaning to life, who seek for a purpose, especially those who have little in this life to bring them comfort, sustenance, and meaning.

The cry goes up 'is this life all there is?' and if so then there are questions of injustice that remain forever unanswered and not dealt with.

---

77   'Doubts and Loves, 2001, Canongate, p.141

The American one-time Bishop of Newark, New Jersey, John Shelby Spong is another who believes very much in compassion, but I would have to say, as with Richard Holloway, this view fails to appreciate the extent and power of love.

John Shelby Spong speaks of all scriptural statements with regard to resurrection as legends, magic, even slight of hand, which he states will never survive in our contemporary world, where miracle and the supernatural are both suspect. "If we insist that Easter's truth must be carried inside a literal framework we doom Easter's truth to the death of irrelevance."[78]

The bodily resurrection of Jesus is a crucial element in understanding the power of love (agape)which is salvation for those who believe it and those who don't, for the present life And beyond.

John Shelby Spong gives the impression that there is only one way to interpret and understand scripture. This is through the lens of what is called 'Midrash'. This understanding I find unacceptable, To hold to this position is to interpret the Bible through the spectacles of folklore, anecdote and legend.

'Midrash' refers to not an exact but a comparative (homiletic) method of exegesis (expounding scripture), a compilation of homiletic teachings or commentaries on the Hebrew Bible in the form of legal, ritual, legendary, moralising, folkloristic and anecdotal parts. While this may have some relevance in some contexts it is certainly

---

78   'Myth and Reality', Harper Collins, p.293

not the only way to understand the texts, and in fact can be misleading. One accepts that John Shelby Spong is a man who wishes to express love as of first importance, as does Richard Holloway; but their approach ignores legitimate interpretations of the Christian faith, which give a valid exegesis of scripture with regard to the resurrection accounts, leading to no other conclusion than acceptance of the bodily resurrection of Jesus.

Professor Emeritus of Systematic Theology of the University of Tubingen, Germany, Jurgen Moltmann, the author of 'Theology of Hope' which has been recognised as one of the most influential works of the last few decades of the 20th century, has written:

"It would be foreign to the intention of the Easter texts themselves if the 'point' of their statements were to be sought solely in the birth of faith. There can be no forbidding the attempt to go behind their kerygma and ask about the reality which underlies their statements and makes them dependable and credible."[79]

Resurrection has been and is held by many millions throughout the world and is a great comfort in times of bereavement, and enables people to live fully in the present with positive hope for the future, but it is not held only because it is a comfort, it is held because it is the truth. Among academics there are those who regard the resurrection of which we speak as giving ultimate relevance to life. Recognising meaning and purpose for the present, coupled with an understanding of human destiny which includes an eternal dimension,who accept the bodily resurrection

---

79 'Theology of Hope', p.161-162

of Jesus, the kind of love Jesus expressed cannot allow humanity to live with such a narrow view of life that excludes the eternal dimension of mystery and miracle.

John Shelby Spong thinks it unnecessary to speculate on the afterlife. He believes the important thing is to live life now. We applaud this concern for life in the present endeavouring to express the compassion of Christ, worked out in the lives of ordinary people, sometimes doing extraordinary things because of this love.

However, the love that Jesus expressed was also very much a love which was keen for people to know the truth of bodily resurrection. Fundamental to the message he wished the disciples to pass on was their testimony to his bodily resurrection. The very first recorded sermon given by Peter at Pentecost, records Peter saying 'God has raised this Jesus to life, and we are all witnesses of the fact'. (Acts 2:32)

The record emphasizes bodily resurrection, when the resurrected Jesus makes a special visit to Thomas who won't believe unless he sees and touches Jesus (John 20:27f), and John in his letter bends over backwards in his eagerness to inform his readers that Jesus, who he describes as the 'Word of Life' is one whom they have seen and touched. He repeats again and again words such as 'that which we have seen and heard, and our hands have touched we declare to you ...' (1 John 1:1-3). And on another occassion Jesus appeared to more than five hundred people at the same time. (1 Corinthians.15:6)

Jesus responds to Thomas and invites him to touch him, feel the wounds of his crucifixion. His love for Thomas is expressed in his desire for Thomas to believe he is the same Jesus who hung on a cross. This is highly significant, Paul writes of Jesus being the 'first born' from the dead (Colossians 1), that is the first to be raised like this, implying we shall also have similar resurrection bodies, recognised by loved ones as the same but different (more of this on the chapter 'Beyond the Horizon').

The bodily resurrection of Jesus has been and is accepted by people from all walks of life, all levels of intelligence. I would maintain it limits the power of love (agape) not to accept the bodily resurrection of Jesus, for it implies that love is hampered by death, that love is limited, that death is a barrier to it. Jesus, in the gospel records and in Paul's letter to the Corinthians, goes out of his way to make it clear this is a 'real' resurrection, not some mystical awakening of faith due to some inner illumination. This would not be any different to many philosophical illuminations.

Tom Wright Theologian observes "… but already in Paul, the resurrection, both of Jesus and then in the future, of his people, is the foundation of the Christian stance of allegiance to a different king, a different lord. Death is the last weapon of the tyrant; and the point of resurrection, despite much misunderstanding, is that death has been defeated. Resurrection is not the re-description of death; it is its overthrow, and with that the overthrow of those whose power depends on it. Despite the sneers and slurs of some contemporary scholars, it was those who believed in the bodily resurrection who were burned at the stake and thrown to the lions. Resurrection was never a way of settling down and becoming respectable, the Pharisees could have told you that. It was the gnostics, who translated resurrection into a private spirituality and dualistic cosmology, thereby more or less altering its meaning into its opposite, who escaped persecution. Which emperor would have sleepless nights worrying that his subjects were reading the *Gospel of Thomas*? Resurrection was always bound to get you in trouble, and regularly did."[80]

The resurrection the disciples witnessed to was an event that declared the victory of love over nature's number one enemy 'death', that which creates meaninglessness. Resurrection declares love creates life worth living; it gives ultimate meaning to the universe and to the individual – more of this later.

Paul states in his letter to the Roman church that there is nothing that can cut a person off from the love of Christ. The love of the Messiah is the love of the one appointed to bring the message of a kingdom not of this world, a kingdom whose foundation is love which while not of this world, operates within this world. It operated on the cross – as we have noted many times in various ways – love that conquered hate – from that cross is the love that is eternal, is victorious over death. So Paul a man who had been eaten up with hate until he met Jesus ,knew the power of love over hate,and thus was able to write,

"… in all things we are more than conquerors through him who loved us. For I am persuaded that neither death, nor life, nor angels, nor principalities, nor powers, nor things present, nor things to come, nor height, nor depth, nor

---

80 'Surprised by Hope', Tom Wright, SPCK, 2007 p.62

any other creature, shall be able to separate us from the love of God, which is in Christ Jesus our Lord." ... and in 1 Corinthians we repeat those lovely words "....faith hope and love,these three things remain, but the greatest of these is love."

Love is about bringing life out of death. It's about making life worth living in the present with a future perspective that transcends death; it's about new beginnings, new creativity, both in the now and beyond, produced by love, in particular that most significant love poured out from a cross, even in death producing life. Such love is indestructible, its power beyond comprehension, its vulnerability, its victory, its relevance, its power in weakness. Ludwig Wittgenstein,the Cambridge philosopher wrote "It is love that believes in resurrection".

This love again and again gives new life and hope to people in the present, it has enabled people to love in the face of death.It brings people together, even enemies in time of war; it survives hatred, no, it is victorious over hatred, as seen in the chapter 'Aspects of Love'. This love, seen in so many vulnerable places, is of such a calibre it moves through life and through death for it is the very essence of real life; people in all cultures recognise real compassionate love when they see it. What is not always recognised is that it is creative of hope that is not limited to earthly life, resurrection is part of its very creativity, resurrection that transcends physical death and produces resurrection bodies, after the pattern of the resurrection body of Jesus of Nazareth risen from the grave – risen and alive having been victorious in extreme vulnerability in dying through the torture of crucifixion.

It is possible to suggest that in order for people who undergo extreme pain, to identify with Jesus, to know he understands severe pain of mind, body and spirit, it was necessary for him to undergo such a death in such a world, as this where crucifixions of one kind or another do take place. It is also necessary from this viewpoint to recognise that the compassion of Jesus was stronger than the pains he endured. It is this compassion that saves from hate that destroys, the love Jesus expressed from a cross brings life. Even when our love falters, his love sees us through as his love saw the disciples through after their desertion and lack of faith.

Death of course is the prelude to resurrection; just as a dying plant drops its seed into the ground (some seed looks like dust, which looks nothing like the plant it came from). From this 'dust', this seed, is produced another plant, recognisable as being the same kind as the one that dropped the seed, yet not the same, this plant is full of new life, not yellowing, wilting, but growing in beauty and maturity into full bloom.

It is important at this juncture to focus on the reality of the death of Jesus, to make clear his death was a real death, thus his resurrection a real resurrection from the dead.

Lee Strobel in his book 'The Case for Easter' examines the crucifixion and resurrection of Jesus of Nazareth in some detail, making it clear Jesus did indeed die, Jesus did indeed rise bodily from the grave. In his book he interviews Dr Metherall, a prominent American physician, former research scientist, who extensively studied the historical, archaeological and medical data concerning the death and resurrection of Jesus of Nazareth. The doctor comments on the beating and crucifixion thus –

"Because of the terrible effects of this beating, there's no question that Jesus was already in a serious to critical condition even before the nails were driven through his hands and feet ... Even before he died, and this is important too, the hypovolemic shock would have caused a sustained rapid heart rate that would have contributed to heart failure, resulting in the collection of fluid in the membrane around the heart, called a pericardial effusion, as well as around the lungs which is called a pleural effusion. Why is this significant? Because of what happened when the soldier came round, and, being fairly certain that Jesus was dead, confirmed it by thrusting a spear into his side ... when the spear was pulled out some fluid, the pericardial effusion and the pleural effusion came out (blood and water) ...

... We are reminded that these soldiers were experts in killing people – that was their job, and they did it very well. They knew without a doubt when a person was dead ... besides, if a prisoner somehow escaped, the responsible soldiers would be put to death themselves, so they had a huge incentive to make absolutely sure that each and every victim was dead when he was removed from the cross."[81]

Commenting on the pathetic condition of Jesus, due to his beating and crucifixion, if it were to have happened as some have suggested, that somehow Jesus survived and somehow was resuscitated by his disciples, Dr Metheral says –

---

81 'The Case for Easter', Lee Strobel, Zondervan, 2003 p.27

"... Listen – a person in that kind of pathetic condition would never have inspired his disciples to go out and proclaim that he's the Lord of Life who triumphed over the grave ... Do you see what I am saying? After suffering that horrible abuse, with all the catastrophic blood loss and trauma, he would have looked so pitiful that his disciples would never have hailed him as a victorious conqueror of death; they would have felt sorry for him and tried to nurse him back to health ... so it's preposterous to think that if he had appeared to them in that awful state, a world movement based on the hope that someday they too would have a resurrection body like his, would have arisen ... there is no way ..."

The last question Lee Strobel puts to Dr Metheral is the 'why?' question. He replies, "So when you ask what motivated him ... well ... I suppose the answer can be summed up in one word – and that word would be *love*."[82]

John Polkinghorne, writes –

"The New Testament is written in the light of its authors' conviction that God raised Jesus Christ from the dead. Without the recognition of that belief, much of its discourse is not fully intelligible."[83]

"All the religious leaders have many things in common. All say wise things; all are credited with remarkable deeds; all have a charismatic power to draw and influence their

82 'The Case for Easter', Lee Strobel, Zondervan, 2003 pp.17,21,24

83 'The God of Hope and the End of the World', SPCK, 2002 p.66

followers. But Jesus is different in a striking way. The others all end their lives in honoured old age, surrounded by faithful disciples who are resolved to carry on the work and message of the master. Jesus dies in mid-life, deserted by his followers, suffering a painful and shameful death that any first century Jew would see as a sign of God's rejection, ...

On the face of it, however promising Jesus' public ministry may appear to have been, in the end it all seems to have ended in failure and disillusionment. If that had been the case, and the story of Jesus ended completely at that grim place of crucifixion, it seems highly likely that he would just have disappeared from history. Yet we have all heard of Jesus, something happened to continue his story, the writers of the New Testament all tell us that it was his resurrection by God on the third day, to live an unending new life of lordship and glory. Can we possibly believe them?"[84]

What we are concerned with here is 'truth'. There are those that would say that no matter how comforting a thought may be, what is the truth? We have just observed how real Jesus of Nazareth's crucifixion and resurrection were. It is crucial to make clear that a Christian understanding of Jesus Christ's crucifixion and resurrection is of an event that took place at a particular time in the history of the world. That Jesus of Nazareth came to his followers in a physical form as the resurrected Jesus, but one not limited to time or space, but none the less physical, a body vital with life, a 'glorified body', to use Paul's phrase.

---

84 'Questions of Faith', Polkinghorne & Beale, p.20-21

Jesus broke down all kinds of barriers, as the resurrected Jesus, he came first to the women, in the society of that time they were not regarded as reliable witnesses, yet the Jewish writer informs us Jesus first appeared to them. The writer is not trying to make this up to prove his point, if he was trying to, he would have had Jesus appearing to the men first. It's reported when the women came with the news 'Jesus is risen', they regarded it as 'idle tales',(Luke24:11) and this is what you would expect from 1st century Jews confronted with such news from women. However we read these words spoken by Jesus, " The first shall be last and the last first."(Matthew19:30) So it was to the women that the risen Christ first came.

Jesus Christ's attitude to the disciples was not to blame those who were borne down with grief, helplessness and fear, whose world had lost its meaning. In fact his love responded to their faithlessness with his faithfulness. His love would bring faith, hope, meaning and purpose back into their lives, to a degree they had not experienced before, for these were to be the pioneers of the early church, which would continue to grow right up to the present day, it is still growing, as it always has somewhere in the world. Worldwide it has never stopped growing whatever difficulties within or without.

Fear drove out the disciples' faith. Jesus' love gave it back to them. His love gave them back their identity and dignity. This love was poured out to a disciple who refused to believe the women's testimony, or the men's testimony to the resurrection, Thomas. This love was poured out to one who denied he even knew Jesus, with curses, when Jesus needed him most, Peter, the one who said he would follow him even to death, (Mark 14:29; Mark 14:71). In fact all the disciple's faith failed.(Matthew.26:27.) Jesus' love was his response, and it gave them back their lives.

Jesus understood what fear of pain and death could do to a human being. It is recorded that he experienced it in Gethsemane when he cried out in agony "let this cup pass from me". (Mark 14:36; Matthew 26:39, 37-38; Luke 22:44).

He prayed that he might not have to face such a death, as he sweated it out in fear, agony and anticipation. Love understands vulnerability, pain, the anticipation of torture and death, and in his own body Jesus could identify with human fear and frailty(the mystery of incarnation).

So from this we comprehend Jesus' understanding of all those who suffer. Understands all those who cannot be heroes, while we thank God for all who are, Jesus understands the weak and the strong. Understands those who loose faith due to their pain, or the pain of others, or the pain of the world, and his response is to declare in his own body, his own pain, that in the vulnerability of love is the power of resurrection; the power of love over hate, which brings life out of death, which gives birth to life before death and after death.This is the love that gives hope to the faithless,life to the lifeless.

Gerald O'Collins commenting on Jesus' attitude to Peter from John's gospel speaks of his reinstatement and commission, his life given back to him through the love of the resurrected Jesus.

"As so often in John's gospel the text invites us to identify with the men and women who meet and experience Jesus.

In this case our identification with the disciples in John 21 entails remembering situations into which we have been drawn right from the first chapter of that gospel. This is an exercise that can recall and heal our own buried past. Peter is taken through all this, down to his shameful failure during the passion. The past is not denied, but recalled, forgiven and lovingly redeemed. A healing through love becomes the basis for Peter's new future ...

Jesus wanted his disciples to be identified by their love, wanted his love to be received by them and passed on by them, producing a witness of love to the world. Our identity as persons is bestowed on us in the love which others have for us ... our identity is equally determined by the love we have for others. In both senses we owe our identity as precious to others."[85]

The love that Peter and those early followers of Jesus were to pass on was the love they had seen in Jesus. A love operating in this world in all kinds of attitudes, words and actions, and a love that continues beyond the grave to express this very same kind of love. The message was of a kingdom whose foundations are love – which is brought to bear in all kinds of present circumstances and which reaches beyond death. It's the message of eternal life in the present, and beyond in resurrection.

It is only such a resurrection message, the physical resurrection of Jesus continuing his ministry beyond the tomb, that could galvanise his followers to the kind of action needed to establish the presence of the kingdom of heaven on earth.

---

85   'Easter Faith', Gerald O'Collins, DLT, 2003, pp.85,97,101

Jesus was fully aware, that what was needed was a 'real' resurrection. The truth is surely not to be found, as Jurgen Moltmann states, in only a birth of faith, however wonderful. One is surely obliged to say, that even before Pentecost (the empowering of the Holy Spirit) there was an event that brought unspeakable joy. There was a joy in their lives that could only be brought about by the occasion of one dearly loved, who they had witnessed die, now alive and well, not a ghost. One who ate a meal with them and who could invite Thomas to touch him, feel the wounds of crucifixion. A solid physical body, but a body not limited by the boundaries of this world, one that could move through time and space!

Jesus declares a resurrection for humanity like his own i.e. a continuance of conscience life beyond the grave. It is vital to make clear that this understanding is one that would most readily be comprehended by the disciples, and indeed I would say by people of any culture by the term 'risen from the dead' (while not comprehending all that Jesus' resurrection means) at the very least all would understand by the term 'risen from the dead' to mean someone who you know and loved now back again with you after death, physically present again.

Love must not only operate within this world, as we have seen, but beyond this world for it to be truly love of the kind the early church described as agape. Love that operates in this world and beyond ,which has ultimate meaning in creation and re-creation. This is the silver lining in life, this is the good news, in life and in death. Love that will not allow humanity to die in meaninglessness, love that having created could not allow death to destroy the value, purpose, meaning of a human being and the universe humanity inhabits. These two things Jesus reminded his disciples of in the gospels, in suffering and resurrection. No matter how much suffering, there is resurrection.

While our minds cannot understand the complexities of life with all its mix of good and bad, it is of the utmost importance that in recognising the resurrection we recognise that the love embodied in Jesus goes on beyond death. Love, while operating wonderfully within this ailing body, is not limited to this body, and there is yet to be even more wonderful manifestations of this love. This love is shown in incredible power in incredible weakness.

With our very limited knowledge of this great mystery, can we not say it was necessary for Jesus to undergo abandonment of such intensity, to declare there is still resurrection, no matter what is flung at us in this world, pain of mind, body or spirit? Thus those in the dark tunnels of forsakenness can know an objective truth, there is resurrection, and even if not knowing it at such a time, there is resurrection. Thus we can say the objective truth of resurrection is of course there, whether it is always subjectively known or not.

"It is important to recognise that in Christian understanding, Jesus' resurrection is the guarantee and foretaste within history of a destiny that awaits all men and women beyond history. Paul told the Corinthians that 'As in Adam all die, so also in Christ shall all be made alive.'"[86]

---

86 'Questions of Truth', John Polkinghorne and Nicholas Beale, WJK, 2009, p.89

Resurrection, it seems to me, is unavoidable when seen in the context of love (agape). We shall now look a little more closely at love beyond the confines of this present earthly stage. Love seen as relevant beyond death as it is before death.Love seen as so vast that the relevance of love in terms of meaning, purpose, fulfilment, exploration, and assurance, cannot be confined to present earthly living only.

The power of the kind of love we have been investigating, which is so relevant to present and future, so bound up with how we view present circumstances. Is so bound up with forgiveness, reconciliation and the victory of love over hate in this world and the next, is beautifully illustrated in the following account which emerged in such a place of horror it is impossible to imagine, as it is impossible to imagine the nightmare of the cross out of which emerged resurrection.

During the Holocaust countless children were exterminated at Ravensbruck concentration camp. When the place was liberated a piece of paper was found, placed with the body of a dead child, on the paper were these words written by an unknown inmate:

"O Lord, remember not only the men and women of good will, but also those of ill will. But do not remember all the suffering they have inflicted on us – remember instead the fruits we have bought, thanks to this suffering: our comradeship, our loyalty, our humility, our courage, our generosity, the greatness of heart which has grown out of all this. And when those who have inflicted suffering on us come to judgment, let all the fruits which we have borne be their forgiveness."[87]

This was a prayer written with an awareness of a future life beyond death, beyond the horizon of present sight, where love would be victorious,. It is to this vast view of life that we now turn, life beyond the horizon.

87   From 'The Hidden Jesus', Donald Spoto, St Martin's Press, 1998

Chapter 5.

Love beyond the horizon, love and human destiny

"**B**elief about the afterlife is not simply a theoretical matter, but one of the most important questions we face alone and together."[88]

It is important, one can say of supreme importance, when investigating belief in the after-life that we come to grips with a concept that breeches the bounds of all that we readily experience in what is called the material world. There are those who find little difficulty in accepting a spiritual dimension to life that includes life after death ,those who can't believe it, those who have some problems in doing so, and those who have no problem at all.

For some, living in this world of technical advance, of increasing knowledge in so many areas of life, find it so all-encompassing that they find it impossible to move beyond it.

---

88 'Imagining Life after Death', Kathleen Fischer, SPCK, 2004-5, p.xi

What is so sad is when some people feel they have arrived at a complete or near-complete understanding of life, so much so that they ridicule any view that espouses a spiritual, eternal view of life. While we are most grateful for all advances that enhance life for good, and which deepens our understanding of life here and in the cosmos, we also realise just how much is still to be explored, and that we are still but touching the edges of the universe.

That many people do accept the concept of a life beyond death is an observable fact worldwide, any anthropologist will concede this when approached as an objective observation.

"Surveys show that many people believe in life after death precisely because they have known love. Love lives in the language of forever. We are reluctant to end a wonderful visit and put a dear friend on a plane bound for home. We drink in the uplifted face of a grandchild and long to see her bloom. Gabriel Marcel said it eloquently, and has been quoted ever since, 'to say that we really love someone is instinctively to insist: Thou, at least, thou shalt not die.'"[89]

Some seem to find it easier to accept nothing beyond what can be measured (in spite of the fact as noted that the microscopic world was not available to us until the advent of the microscope). Some cannot seem to conceive of anything that could transcend the dissolution of the body and enter a dimension of life that has no barriers to its everlasting experience of 'being'. For such it is easier to say, 'when we are dead, we are dead', there is nothing more.

---

89   Ibid. pp.104-105

That one could say is the easy thing to believe, and refusing to explore any further.

Certainly with such a belief one could opt out. It could be said it would be easier for us to remain earthbound and not to venture into space, but we have, into that vastness that appears to have no end. It is also true that if we limit research to our place in the cosmos to the purely biological, and fail to take up the challenge to go beyond biological barriers, we fail to appreciate the truly vastness of life.

"From ancient times to modern times, a common thread runs through the literature of hope: the incompleteness of what we now know when compared with what is to come. Examples large and small of our limited perceptions abound. There are colours we cannot see, and sounds we do not hear, because we are simply not equipped to do so. Even physicists are unable to picture all the dimensions of space. Depictions of the after-life anticipate the fulfilment not only of heart, but of mind as well. We will be more fully aware …

… A friend whose daily meditation practice comes from the Buddhist tradition talks about her conviction that death will lead to greater awareness. This belief does not take away her sense of separation and grief when someone dies, she says, or her shrinking from the pain and diminishment of the dying process: It does take away my fear though, because I think we experience more awareness of all aspects of life after death. I cannot say I know this intellectually but I sense it profoundly. This veil will lift after death, revealing what has been hidden"[90]

---

90   Ibid. pp.38-39

What I suggest is revealed is the answer to life which is in fact partially revealed now but which is so vast it inevitably goes beyond our present horizons. This is that creative energy, 'Love', which brings meaning to all things.

"Love alone prevails when everything else has been withered by the pitiless inroads of time, decay and death. Carl Jung's oft-quoted observation that amongst his older patients there was no case of philosophical ill health that was not ultimately related to a search for a deeper religious meaning to life (Collected works XI, para 509), is crucial to our preparation for death. Only as we ponder the deep things of God will we come to the core of our own mortality."[91]

Etty Hillesum came to know this in her own experience – this deeper inner self, and she came to know this pondering on the deep things of God, while living in Nazi occupied Amsterdam, and she did indeed come to the core of her own mortality.

"She consciously nourishes a profound inner freedom. And at the heart of this rigorously disciplined inner life was her openness to the mystery of the Divine experienced within her as vulnerable presence. It was this that fortified her refusal to hate."[92]

This inner self, we can say, is that which the real self is. While that grey convoluted mass, which is the brain, while

---

91   'Life Eternal', Martin Israel, SPCK, 1993 p.37

92   'Etty Hillesum, A Life Transformed', Patrick Woodhouse, Continuum, 2009 pp.51-53. Reproduced by kind permission of Continuum International Publishing Group. Reproduced by kind permission of Continuum International Publishing Group.

truly wonderful, is, looking at it, surely not all there is to me; a mass of grey matter, 'ME'! The inner 'power', is that which was brought increasingly alive in Etty Hillesum and those others mentioned in these pages and many throughout history, which lives in the present and which transcends death. And Etty comes to the conclusion at the end of her first two letters as to what it is that gives this life. It is That which transcends hate, that which is the only true response to hate, which introduces one to beauty even in the midst of ugliness, and which brings life even out of death ...which is constructive not destructive .

"I know that those who hate have good reason to do so. But why should we always have to choose the cheapest and easiest way? It has been brought home forcibly to me here how every atom of hatred added to the world makes it an even more inhospitable place. And I also believe, childishly perhaps, but stubbornly, that the earth will become more habitable again only through the love that the Jew Paul described to the citizens of Corinth in the thirteenth chapter of his letter."[93]

That letter of course being the famous letter which highlights that love which is even greater than faith, and which is eternal.

It is because Etty discovered her real inner self that she began to appreciate life even in the transit camp, even in the concentration camp, even with life expectancy in such a place so limited, an appreciation of life even without the material benefits of life. Etty thus had an appreciation of that life within which transcends death, an appreciation of life which gave her a sense of freedom even in captivity and which enabled her to

---

93   Ibid. p.75

live increasingly to the full in the present, even in the face of impending death, because this life transcends death, is not limited by the material world, is not limited by death. It was this life that Maximillian Kolbe communicated to others in the death block enabling them to live again even in the face of death– and the name of this life is love (agape).

While many people recognise that love, in terms of understanding, compassion, mercy, forgiveness, togetherness, is what enriches life, not all recognise that depth of love which is not confined to our present mode of existence. This is often due to the influence of the material world, as we have observed, when life is seen as being all to do with the present, and increasing instant gratification.

"Because of our culture of consumerism and its offer of instant gratification the experience of linear time (i.e. having to wait for one thing to follow another) is fading – the present is all. So any sense of a beyond, any sense of 'after' fades with it."[94]

"Belief in an after-life has been too often packaged with discredited and incredible images of life beyond death. Bizarre second comings of Christ, lurid details of heaven and hell. As such, it has been hard to retain belief in an after-life itself, apart from those wider images. All these are reasons why the belief has declined. ... Even if a belief does take wing in the context of some mortal fear or mortal longing, which of itself does not mean the belief is necessarily wrong. My fear of death and ache for mortality does not mean there's no such thing as an after-life, any more than fear of hunger and an ache for food means there is no such thing as food."[95]

---

94   'Sacred and Secular', Michael Ramsey, Longman, 1965 p.11

95   'Life Beyond Death', Vernon White, DLT, 2006 pp.14-15

Karl Rahner,in 1984 at the age of eighty in Freiburg, his birthplace, gave his last lecture of any substance, he concluded that lecture with a peroration about death and the after-life, in which he says,

"When then our life so far, however long it has been, appears only as a simple, short explosion of our freedom that previously presented itself to us stretched out in slow motion, an explosion in which question has become answer, possibility reality, time eternity, and freedom offered freedom accomplished; when then we are shown in the monstrous shock of a joy beyond saying that this monstrous silent void, which we experience, as death, is in truth filled with the originating mystery that we call God, with God's light and with God's love that receives all things and gives all things; and when then, out of this pathless mystery, the face of Jesus, the blessed one, appears to us, and this specific reality is the divine surpassing of all that we truly assume regarding the past- all- graspness of the pathless God – then, then I don't want actually to describe anything like this, but nevertheless, I do want to stammer out some hint of how a person can for the moment expect what is to come: by experiencing the very submergence that is death as already the rising of what is coming. Eighty years is a long time. But for all of us, the lifetime assigned to us is the short moment in which what is meant to be comes to be."[96]

Dr Kubler-Ross in her autobiography "traces the events that shaped her intellectually and spiritually, and inevita-

---

96 'Expressions of a Catholic Theologian'from Karl Rahner,spiritual writings Ed.Philip Endean,Orbis.2004.p.203.

bly led her to explain her ultimate truth – that death does not exist but a transformation."[97]

Love is concerned with bringing into life a meaning which enables one to live fully. Love is interested in the fullness of life, this includes life that is so 'full' it overflows into eternity; and this life is <u>the</u> life within a 'being', one that is not limited to the outward material body. This is not to say some may not loose touch with this inner reality, but that does not mean it cannot be regained,. And those with any number of physical mental or spiritual disabilities still have an inner life that can develop which has within it the desire to live and love.For all of us,we can say, it can be recognized and developed here and in the hereafter.

I well remember over a period of some two years communicating with a young man, who could not speak and could not walk and had no coordination in his arms and legs. I did not always know how much he was taking in, as I talked to him on a number of subjects, reading from a variety of books on all kinds of topics.

One day I was talking about life being bigger than we can ever possibly imagine. I spoke of the vastness of space, the dimension of the universe; then went on to include the eternal dimension of life. That there was within us a life, that no matter what our external circumstances, no matter what was going on with our bodies, there was this inner life and that there was an eternity of being where we had new

---

97 'The Wheel of Life, a memoir of living and dying', Bantam Press London, originally published 1997, Scribner New York, USA, quoted in David Hodges 'Do we survive death', published by David Hodges with Pilgrim Trust, 2004, 2nd edition, p.88

glorified bodies. This was the general pattern, and I almost took a step back as I experienced something I could not remember ever having experienced before. His face shone, he burst forth in a glorious smile that lit up his whole face, a look of delight, of such magnitude I find it difficult to find words to express. That light, that light within him, was recognising and responding to that eternal dimension of life, beyond the horizon, beyond this present scene, that is how it communicated to me.

Harry Patch came to believe in life after death during the First World War....

"We came across a lad from A Company. He was ripped open from his shoulder to his waist by shrapnel, and lying in a pool of blood. When we got to him, he looked at us and said, 'shoot me'. He was beyond all human help, and before we could draw a revolver, he was dead. And the final word he uttered was 'Mother!' I was with him in the last seconds of his life. It wasn't a cry of despair; it was a cry of surprise and joy. I think – although I wasn't allowed to see her, I am sure – his mother was in the next world to welcome him and he knew it. I was just allowed to see that much, and no more. Yet I'm positive that when he left this world, wherever he went, his mother was there, and from that day I've always remembered that cry, and that death is not the end."[98]

The whole concept of an after-life has been well researched by Dr David Hodges a biological scientist he states,

---

[98] Harry Patch wrote this for his book published 2007 when he was 109 years of age.

"The history of science provides many examples of theories apparently explaining how the world works which have had, ultimately, to be discarded or severely modified, as a result of subsequent discoveries. The final decision as to whether or not we accept the reality of survival must be an inner individual choice. It will be based on personal experience, but supported by the work and experience of others. Thus, we are given the choice between:

The outwardly bleak, meaningless and mechanistic outlook of the materialist, humanist interpretation of life – with, for me, its lack of any clear justification for this approach. Or the positive, meaningful, and life-affirming philosophy of the spiritual hypothesis.

I find myself very much supporting the latter. Particularly as it is reinforced by a large body of direct and frequently explicit evidence.

At least the life-affirming hypothesis gives me a spiritual philosophy by which to live. It provides a meaning to life. It leads to an explanation for, and understanding of many of the events in life which otherwise may seem pointless and incomprehensible.

The information which has come from research into survival provides humanity with the means and the justification to plot a more constructive and positive way ahead, rather than the blind and destructive path that we have been following for the past two or three hundred years. So, when seeking to come to a decision we need to consider what I have termed, "the most important question",.....the most important question in life, because so much hangs on the answer is:

Which view of the universe, the spiritual approach or the material approach, best describes reality, and which is redundant?

I suggest that the evidence for survival provides a sound basis for an answer in favour of the spiritual approach to life"[99]

Thus in this work we have observed events that spoke into life of that love that has its roots in eternity, in creative love that expresses itself in the present even in the darkest moments, giving glimpses of that which sees life that transcends the present, while being very much in the present, even in the paradoxes of life.

If we recognise love is behind creation, then we can move on to appreciate it is love that will see us through this life on into the next. No! not just see us through but enable us to live in the present with meaning and purpose, even when a dearly loved one has died; for in recognition, even if not in full acceptance, that there is life beyond the horizons of this life, there is given birth to a hope which when developed can remind us of the unifying power of love, this is an eternal power, no matter how weak or strong our faith may or may not be, this love has eternal unifying power. In fact we can say this Love(God)believes in us, even if we don't believe in Him,

Whatever our glimpses, understanding of love here, however big, however small, they are all enveloped and expanded in a love that meets us beyond death, having

---

99 Do we survive death? – David Hodges, David Hodges with Pelegrin Trust 2004 – p120-121

seen us through it. I admire the strength which some atheists have shown in the face of impending death, but this question of human destiny is not only about my personal survival, it is about the whole business of life with a capital 'L'. It's about the life of the whole universe, it's about accountability, it's about meaning and purpose, it's about putting right what is wrong .

This love (agape) is the answer to our individual lives, and the life of the universe. This love is of such a quality it will bring salvation ultimately to the whole cosmos. It will bring salvation to the Richard Dawkins and the Bertrand Russells of this world, for the very reason that when all else fails, love will emerge victorious. For all of us fail to some degree in comprehension, in justice, mercy, compassion, etc. But this love will enable us to develop in maturity if not here, then beyond the horizon; for this love, as already observed, is not a slave to death, to find death a barrier.

While some express the view they would prefer annihilation to conscious life beyond death, many do not find much comfort in this, and for the bereaved holding to such a belief can make life appear pointless. Again human destiny is not only about ourselves, how well we face or do not face death.Its about "meaning" for us and the whole cosmos.

A view of annihilation has nothing to say about unfulfilled lives. Some have been privileged to have lives full of meaning and purpose, though some of these have wanted more time for this and that, to finish some project or take up the challenge of another (for others, it's solely a matter to try to stay alive). Some would like more time to see children or grandchildren grow to maturity, etc.So what of the many who die with unfulfilled lives, some even only just having started out in life, some hardly having left the womb, or even still in it.

The cry that goes up so often is a cry for meaning. There has always been a concern to discover our human destiny, in both temporal and eternal terms. It includes questions concerned with evil, suffering, and value. And whatever obstacles to understanding are cast in the way, the need for answers is an eternal cry.

"We are haunted by the need to make sense of things. There are many great accounts of our origin and destiny, and countless explanations of how the world is as we find it. Some argue that it is impossible to make an informed choice, and commend neutrality in all such issues. Yet a cynic might argue that this is little more than a refusal to engage with the great issues of life, draped for the sake of intellectual decency with some rather skimpy shreds of relativist philosophy."[100]

While some give up on any meaning for the universe, most at least want to discover a meaning for their own lives. The whole question then becomes very personal. This then translates to how one views others, how one views daily living. Meaningless living (existence) can escalate into a bleak negative view of life which can infect those around us. Some could say even if there were no life after death, there is still purpose in living for others, 'love your neighbour as yourself. Self-worth and recognition of another's worth. But this still leaves big questions regarding justice and the meaning of a universe with its mixture of good and bad. A

---

100 'Glimpsing the Face of God', Alistair McGrath, Lion, 2002 p.36

life beyond the horizons of this life posits a dimension where all is put right.

Humanity longs for meaning, not only for the present, but as regards the meaninglessness of the dissolution of the body, for dissolution into chemical residue has no meaning in personal conscience life lived and relationships forged. We are made for each other.

Professor Hans Kung quoting Ernst Bloch writes:

"The infinite longing of a man is restless, unfinished, never fulfilled, continually starting out afresh, continually longing, learning, seeking, continually reaching out for what is different and new – has nevertheless a meaning and does not eventually end in a void. Hans Kung comments – if there is consummation in eternal life, then I have the justified hope – contrary to Sigmund Freud's atheistic fears that 'the oldest, strongest and most urgent wishes of mankind are not all illusions, but eventually fulfilled.'"[101]

John Polkinghorne comments, "Belief in human destiny beyond death stems not only from the value of individual creatures but also from the recognised incompleteness of our lives in this world. All of us will die with business unfinished, hurts unhealed, potentialities unrealised. The vision of continuing process of purification leading to the inexhaustible experience of the vision of the living God, as set out in Dante's Purgatorio and Paradiso, is a necessary part of the fulfilment which alone makes total sense of the assertion of individual value. I cannot think that mere

---

101 'Eternal Life', Collins, 1984 (English) p.286

remembrance, such as process theologies notion of our lives contributing to the filling of the reservoir of divine experience, is an adequate account. It confuses the preservation of the past with the perfection of the future and it gives a diminished description of God's love for Abraham, Isaac and Jacob, for you and for me."[102]

I am the God of Abraham, Isaac and Jacob, I am the God of the living, not of the dead, quotes Jesus to the Sadducees, who did not believe in resurrection. Matthew chapter 22, verse 32.Thus Jesus refers to Abraham, Isaac and Jacob as still living!

It is true that there are theological complexities just as there are scientific perplexities. Vernon White has observed there are philosophical warrants for the assumption i.e. our capacity to think beyond direct experience.

"These appear chiefly in idealist philosophy, though I cannot pursue that here. There are even some kinds of warrants in recent science. In its references to quantum fields and subatomic realities, science is now attempting to talk of invisible realities beyond direct experience. It thinks it can do so because these other realities beyond experience leave a sort of trail of effects within our experience. This is at least an analogy of the 'trail of the holy' in this world. It mirrors the way that glimpses of God's transcendence and eternity are picked up in their effects, even if not directly perceived."[103]

---

102 'Belief in God in an Age of Science, Yale University Press, 1998 p.23

103 'Life beyond Death', L.T.D., 2006

Kathleen Fischer draws our attention to the scientist Russell Stannard. She writes, "Many scientists themselves affirm the existence of more than they can see. Russell Stannard, head of the physics department at the Open University in London, describes how his own field of high-energy nuclear physics exemplifies this. He researches the behaviour of subatomic particles too small to be seen directly. Because they are invisible, it is necessary to draw inferences from observing their effects. The particles usually leave a trail – like a string of bubbles in a transparent liquid – marking where they have been. As these subatomic particles collide with each other, or spontaneously disintegrate, they create characteristic patterns that mark the path they followed …"

Kathleen Fischer continues, drawing attention to Paul Davies, Professor of Mathematical Physics at the University of Adelaide in Australia,

"He notes that we cannot kick, see, or smell everything we trust, as though it were some kind of concrete block. Atoms are too tiny to see or touch directly. The same is true of quantum fields, which are indistinct configurations of invisible energy. Davies believes modes of knowing that are different from the scientific apply to many things in ordinary life: music, mathematics, information, thoughts, and emotions.

This way of knowing the invisible from the effects it produces is not so unlike the way each of the major religious traditions judges genuine religious experience. Authentic relationship with the Holy leaves a trail. It is a path marked by compassion. As the prophet Muhammad said, 'Do you love your creator? Love your fellow beings first.'"[104]

Events we have observed in this work spoke into life of the love that has its roots in eternity, in creative love that expresses itself in the present even in the darkest moments, giving glimpses of that which sees life that transcends the present while being very much experienced in the present.

In science and religion we are dealing with immense questions, how things work, how this or that is possible, why things are as they are. It is not surprising that people raise all kinds of questions when faced with the question of human destiny as being that which goes beyond this present scene. What of people blown to bits; how can the bodies of the dead be reconstructed even if not blown to bits in some disaster, for all bodies are burnt to ashes or rot and dissolve into the elements of the earth. And there are bodies that are vaporised in terrible events like Hiroshima and Nagasaki.

John Blanchard writing a book on human destiny with which I strongly disagree as regards his view on hell, never the less offers a helpful illustration regarding 'the body' in respect of its eternal destiny. He writes:

"To die is not to be beyond God. A teacher may write a word with his chalk on the blackboard and then rub it off. But that does not preclude him from writing that same word again. It should not surprise us that God is able to rewrite that bundle of genetic and psychological informa-

---

104 'Imagining Life after Death', SPCK, 2005 pp.4-5

tion which is us, and draw us again on the blackboard of life after we have died. The Bible gives us no detailed explanation of this process, and tells us merely that human bodies, which were created to live in time, will be modified in some way to live in eternity, while retaining their individual and unique identities ... (John Blanchard then goes on to tell us)....questions about reassembly of the bodies of the dead are foolish as God created the entire universe out of nothing in the first place – he simply 'spoke and it came to be' (Psalm 33:9). Why should it be any problem to him to do whatever will be necessary to raise from the dead as living beings bodies that had disintegrated and to all intents and purposes disappeared? As John Calvin wrote 'Since God has all the elements at his disposal, no difficulty can prevent him from commanding the earth, the fire and the water to give up what they seem to have destroyed.'"[105]

"Christian teaching does not rely on the immortality of the soul, but on the transformation of the whole person. Death is real. But we believe that God will not forget us; everlastingly God remembers us. While developing a new way to speak of soul, Polkinghorne insists it is reasonable to hope that the pattern that is me will be remembered by God, and re-created in a new environment of God's making. Because God will not abandon the Universe, the matter of the world to come will be the transformed matter of this world. This is the full realisation of the age-old language of prophetic hope.

---

105 'Whatever happened to hell' Evangelical Press, 1993 pp.96-97 ... For my arguments against John Blanchard's view of hell, see my 'Hell – Fact or Fiction?', Athena Press, 2006

O dwellers in the dust awake and sing for joy! For your dew is a radiant dew and the earth will give birth to those long dead. (Isaiah 26:19)

This is the message of Jesus' empty tomb. The resurrection of the body is not the resuscitation of our present structure. It is liberation from that decay, into a new kind of personhood."[106]

The reason 'why' God will not forget us is understood when we see ourselves made in God's image. We do not forget the ones we <u>love</u> in life or in death – they are always remembered. And God has the ability to keep us in relationship now and always. For God in the love of agape will not forget us ,the love of Agape is everlasting.

Belief in an after-life gives meaning to human existence. Without a belief in an after-life injustices are never addressed, things are not ultimately put right. People cry out for justice. Sadly it has to be said compassion is often ruled out of justice. There are those who have treated their fellow human beings with contempt, or as a means to an end; there are those who have abused their power, who have tortured, killed without any apparent remorse. Some terrible things have been done in the name of a law, but without compassion. Love is concerned with compassion, is compassion. Judgement in the context of love is about transforming lives from the bad to the good, wrong to right.

"Down through the centuries it is possible to trace two distinct strands of political thought which diverge over

---

106 Imaging Life After Death.Kathleen Fischer.

precisely this fundamental issue of jurisprudence. On the one hand there are advocates of what is called, 'Positive Law'. For them, law is a branch of science, a system of statutes resting on the absolute legislative authority of the state. It should be invulnerable to prejudice or circumstance, as predictable as the law of gravity, and just as inexorable....

.....On the other hand are the advocates of 'natural law', for whom law is a branch of ethics. They emphasise the principle of equity rather that the strict letter of the law.(Roy Clements goes on to comment)..... it used to be the function of the courts of chancery under the Lord Chancellor to see that equity or fairness always prevailed.....there is now little room to redress grievances arising from intrinsic inequities in the law itself."[107]

The basis of natural law is simply, yet profoundly, 'love', which brings about fairness .This love this compassion, is the very quality Bertrand Russell said was the answer (see chapter one, page one) to those obstacles that stand in the way of human progress.

Russell also said, "Nothing can penetrate the loneliness of the human heart except the highest intensity of the sort of love the religious teachers have preached."[108]

This compassion is the crucial element in ultimate justice. So that the inequalities of life are finally addressed, with a justice that operates according to the very best of natural law because it will be worked out in the context of agape

---

107 'Practising Faith in a Pagan World', Roy Clements, p.97, 120

108 'There is a God', Antony Flew, Harper One, 2007 p,xxi

love, that which seeks what is best for all on earth will find its completion in ultimate wholeness beyond the horizon, when all things are worked out to completion.

This completion is the result of that love that Jesus expressed on the cross, pouring out his compassion to the last, forgiving his enemies. And when we remember his words to love one's neighbour as oneself, valuing others and ourselves, and loving enemies, how can one conceive of a destiny beyond death that includes a place of eternal punishment, as preached and expounded by some, a form of punishment which has no remedial content?

Agape love cannot therefore envisage a human destiny which includes a place of everlasting punishment, worse than even the horrors of concentration camps. Such an understanding of human destiny is to believe in the defeat of love. This understanding is surely foreign to the understanding in 1 Corinthians 13 which states love never ends and love never fails.

Jurgen Moltmann has commented, "Judgement is not God's last word. Judgement establishes in the world the divine righteousness on which the new creation is to be built. But God's last word is 'Behold I make all things new' (Revelation 21:5). From this no-one is excepted. Love is God's compassion with the lost. Transforming grace is God's punishment for sinners. It is not the right to choose that defines the reality of human freedom. It is the doing of the good."[109]

---

109 'God will be All in All', 1999, ed Richard Bauckham, T&T Clark

It is strange that while some scholars will find ways of seeing some passages of scripture, that on the face of it are explicit on certain matters, but which when understood in the way they should be viewed in the context of their time and place e.g. women keeping silent in the church, blaspheming the Holy Spirit, women covering their heads, war in the Old Testament and so forth are seen in the context of their culture and literary style et cetera, have not exercised this with the same vigour as regards hell. Where they seem bent on holding to a doctrine of eternal punishment. It would seem far more in keeping with the general ethos of the ministry of Jesus to understand that God will not even take man's 'no' for a final answer on the matter, as if human beings have the final say as to their destiny! As Jurgen Moltmann points out.

Love, according to 1 Corinthians 13, 'never gives up'. This fits in well with Jesus' parables in Luke 15, of the lost sheep, son and coin. This love woos humanity to a realisation of salvation. Martin Luther, the great reformer, wrote, "God forbid that I should limit the time for acquiring faith to the present life; in the depths of divine mercy there may be opportunity to win it in the future state ..."[110]

Jurgen Moltmann commenting on human 'free will' writes ...

"The logic of hell seems to me not merely inhumane but also extremely atheistic: here the human being in his freedom of choice is his own lord and god. His own will

---

[110] 'Letter to Hans von Rechenberg' 1523 (Luthers Briefe, ii 454) quoted in appendix 'Hell – Fact or Fiction?', David Clayton, Athena Press, 2006

is his heaven – or his hell. God is merely the accessory who puts that will into effect. If I decide for heaven, God must put me there; if I decide for hell, he has to leave me there. If God has to abide by our free decision, then we can do with him what we like. Is that 'the love of God'? Free human beings forge their own happiness and are their own executioners. They do not just dispose over their lives here; they decide on their eternal destinies as well. So they have no need of any God at all. After a God has perhaps created us free as we are, he leaves us to our fate. Carried to this ultimate conclusion, the logic of hell is secular humanism, as Feuerbach, Marx and Nietzsche already perceived a long time ago."[111]

The love of the creator is not thwarted by death (Job 42:2 we read 'no plans of yours can be thwarted). It is God's plan that salvation is for the world, that all things will be made new. As we read in Revelation chapter 21 in the Christian scriptures,

"Then I saw a new heaven and a new earth … He will wipe every tear from their eyes. There will be no more death, or mourning or crying or pain, for the old order of things has passed away. He who was seated on the throne said, 'I am making everything new!' Then he said, 'write this down, for these words are trustworthy and true.'"[112]

Love enables one to live in a hope for the future which is based on the certain expression of love that is everlasting.

---

111 Quoted in 'Hell – Fact or Fiction?', p.96, and found in 'God will be All in All'.p.45.ed.Richard Bauckham.

112 Revelation 21:1, 4-5, N.I.V.

The message of the crucified Christ is crucial in understanding that not only death, but even the worst kind of death, is not a barrier to new life. The message of hope centred in love, in that particular kind of love, that loves even enemies from a cross, is also a message that informs us in the tortured body of Jesus of Nazareth that not even the worst of suffering can prevent this love from doing its work; however incomprehensible, however many unanswerable questions there are this side of eternity, this love will continue the work begun in the decades of history before Christ, climaxing in the crucified body of Jesus, continuing on in the decades after Christ. Declaring its power to work even in the worst of impossible situations until it works to a consummation of history, in the total victory of vulnerable love, (declared even in the strength of weakness[113]) in a new heaven and a new earth.

But there is something more that is being worked out in the present, but which is part of eternity as is the work of love in crucifixion; and without which one cannot talk of crucifixion. It is of course as we have noted , resurrection; there is no crucifixion without resurrection, and no resurrection without crucifixion.

While some would limit this work of love in crucifixion and resurrection to a particular tradition or rule of faith in order to qualify for its validity in one's life, thus limiting its scope, we must I feel see its power of compassion in reaching out to all and ultimately encompassing all in total victory over all forces of darkness. As Jesus reached out with his love from the cross to his followers and to his

---

113 A phrase used as the title of Roy Clement's book, 'The Strength of Weakness', Christian Focus, 1994

murderers. And as in the parable of the lost son, spoken to those who were planning to kill him, represented by the older son in the story, who the father goes out to, and whose love encompasses him with the words of inclusion, "but my son, everything I have is yours." (Luke 15) Both sons were welcomed into the home.

Jesus, with the wounds of crucifixion but in resurrection power, in a resurrection body, comes to his disciples. There is a resurrection power at work in the present, and one can say an aspect of this is its power to work even in times of deepest loss, and feelings of desperation; a power that reminds us we are made for eternity. That all our hopes for life are not groundless, for we are made in the image of the eternal creator; when that image is clouded over, the power of love can still bring it to fruition in resurrection. This light of love is inextinguishable.

We quote again from John's gospel (chapter 1, verse 5) "The light shines in the darkness. The darkness has never put it out. The darkness has not understood it." (can be-Translated both ways). This has proved true, in the lives of those who discover the kind of love we have looked at, not understood as yet, but giving life again and again even in situations of 'living death' – this is the love enigma!

The discovery of 'this love' is also discovery of 'meaning'. This is illustrated again in the life of Etty Hillesum .

"Surrounded in this camp by so many 'bundles of human misery' desperate and unable to face life, she felt that she had what was needed for the huge task of giving support: a deep well of compassion in her heart, and skills in the art of listening. At the heart of her vocation to care was her confidence in the inner meaning she had found.

The psychotherapist Victor Frankl, who survived Auschwitz, wrote that in such extremes, when everything is stripped away, people can only survive if they have discovered meaning ... Etty Hillesum discovered a meaning that filled her full of love, And a conviction that even in that place in those times God was found love was present. In one sentence she sums up her deepest passion ... 'there must be someone to live through it all and bear witness to the fact that God lived, even in these times.'"[114]

And there were others such as Maria Skobtsova, ,a nun in Ravensbruch concentration camp, who bore such a witness. It was two communists, eye witnesses who testified ... "with no vested interest in fabricating such a story, to the fact that she went voluntarily to martyrdom, in order to help her companions to die."

Victor Frankl wrote,

"We who lived in concentration camps can remember the men who walked through the huts comforting others, giving away their last piece of bread. They may have been few in number, but they offer sufficient proof that everything can be taken from a man but one thing: the last of human freedoms – to choose ones attitude in any given set

---

114 'Etty Hillesum, a life transformed' pp.100-101. Reproduced by kind permission of Continuum International Publishing Group. Reproduced by kind permission of Continuum International Publishing Group.

of circumstances, to choose ones way. (Man's search for meaning)[115]

This all points to a love (compassion) that is the power of resurrection in the present, giving life even in death, this resurrection which stems from that love of Calvary, which is also that which brings in the resurrection of humanity beyond the dissolution of the body, and which brings in the resurrection of the whole cosmos, a new heaven, new earth.

At this point it will be helpful to turn again to the writing of John Polkinghorne

He writes of the old creation and the new creation, we have been observing how love works constantly in the old creation in weakness declaring power, the power of compassion even in the face of death, a love victorious and which will bring about wholeness for the universe – the love which takes us beyond the horizon.

Polkinghorne writes of the old and new creation in this way –

"Our best clue to how these twin conditions of continuity/ discontinuity might be satisfied is given us by the event that is our main source of insight into God's ultimate purpose of creation, the resurrection of Jesus Christ. It is Jesus himself who lives again and whose body still bears the scars of his passion. Here is continuity. Yet he is not just revived for another spell of earthly life, for he is alive for evermore, risen and glorified, and his body can appear and disappear in locked rooms. Here is discontinuity.

115 'Candles in the Dark', Mary Craig, Hodder, 1984 p.99

The resurrection of Jesus on the third day is the great seed event from which the new creation has already begun to grow. The worlds of the old and new creations exist, in some sense, 'side by side' today, so that reality has the in-between character of a mixture of 'already and not yet'. However, eventually the whole of the old will be transformed into the new. This redemptive unfolding of the new creation is a great act of divine power and love, bringing about the completion of God's purposes.... so it is the coming of the new creation that makes fully intelligible God's purpose in bringing the present world into being."[116]

---

116 'Living with Hope, a scientist looks at Advent, Christmas and Epiphany', SPCK, 2003 p.97

Chapter 6.

Summing up

John Lennox regarding the enigmas of the building bricks of life has written, "It is hard for us to get any kind of picture of the seething dizzyingly complex activity that occurs inside a living cell, which contains within its lipid membrane maybe 100 million proteins of 20,000 different types and yet the whole cell is so tiny that a couple of hundred could be placed on the dot in this letter 'i'"[117]

Realising the complexity of life in both macro and micro worlds which we have looked at in this work, and realising the complexity of human beings, it is not surprising that we come to the limit of our understanding at any given time, this is especially so when we try to comprehend the author of life, who started the whole thing in the first place. This author in Christian terms is understood as love –

When we understand love as the key to understanding our meaning and purpose and our roots in some kind of eternal love, there will be points at which we are bound to flounder. W.H. Vanstone writes –

---

117 'God's Undertaker', Lion, 2007 p.117

" … We may approximate to a description of authentic love as limitless as precarious and as vulnerable. None of these three epithets is precise or wholly free from ambiguity and we should be glad to use words more simple and exact. But perhaps this is not possible, for our description of authentic love is not a description of something which is commonly, or even occasionally, seen, felt or experienced: it is extrapolation or approximation for the shape of our practical power of discrimination …..

….., we can approximate towards that which is sought towards that which love 'ought to be'. It is perhaps proper that our approximation should contain a degree of mistiness and imprecision; for we are describing not that which many a man has known or experienced but that towards which every man, at the depth of his being which is more profound than language, gropes and aspires."[118]

When this immense love is exercised it is thus a miracle when love of enemy is actually given concrete expression. We have seen in these pages something of this miracle. We have seen that deep down there is within humanity at its best a desire for togetherness even with ones enemies, as we noted in 'the truce' of 1914-15 in the midst of war. We observed this love expressed in such ways it is difficult if not impossible to comprehend in all its depth. So we observe this love is inexpressible in words, and when it is actually expressed in life it is indeed an enigma.

This love has within it the power of resurrection both in giving life to the lifeless in the present (i.e. Maximillian

---

118 'Love's Endeavour, Love's Expense', pp.53-54

Kolbe, Etty Hillesum etc) but also a life beyond the death of this body.

This love while including miraculous expressions here , goes beyond all our experience in this world, it transcends death, thus it is beyond computation, it's bound to be for we find it difficult enough if not impossible to describe the building blocks of our physical life and its origin. It goes beyond what we can fully comprehend in the present, though we have made some attempt in the chapter 'Beyond the Horizon'.

This love which we have been looking at is indestructible. When at certain times in history it would be considered so black as being beyond hope, the light has pierced through the darkness again and again, when it would appear it would be impossible for it to do so. Not always removing the circumstances but enabling life to be present, one could say, in deep pulsating effectiveness, as we have seen in these pages, we could say an even greater miracle than having the problem removed.

Now we have noted this love-motivated life has an eternal dimension to it. If there were no life after death then the incredible suffering that there is in this world could lead one to the conclusion of meaninglessness. Those who suffer unremittingly, who have little or no happiness in this life, who even die in misery, is that it? Is one left with nothing but a negative view, a narrow view of life that leaves no room for the ultimate renewal of creation?

Consider the following comment, "An Atheistic view has been expressed something like this... Death is certain and this is all there is. All is centered in this life with its mixture of good and bad, beauty and mystery, pain, joy, sadness, securities and insecurities, love, laughter and tears, one falls and one gets up this is all there is and this is all one wants."[119] Sadly this does not appear to consider the marginalized.

There are those in our world who desperately want something 'more' because their life is not a balanced mixture of joy, loneliness and love, and there are those in the so-called third world who want not something more, just 'something', for they have 'nothing'. And there are those with mental conditions who even in the midst of western affluence feel they have 'nothing'. And if one accepts there is mystery in life, how then can one in the same breath state 'there is nothing more'. This is not a good reasonable even scientific conclusion, or religious one, for true religion, true science and spirituality, seek to discover more and more truth about ourselves and the world we live in. This statement seems to close the door to any further exploration for meaning for truth, and very little awareness of the marginalised on this planet.

As already stated in these pages this is not only about 'me' as an individual, it is that, but much more, it is about ultimate justice, about all things being put right. While this life may be alright for us, and for some, it is not so for everyone – by a long way.

Does the unending cycle of disease, war, pointless bloodshed, misunderstanding, wickedness, abuse, cruelty, have to go on? If this were the end of the story, it is indeed as black as it could possibly be. While there are big questions

---

119 Unable to locate the source

we do not now have the answers to, such as why should there be suffering, on such a scale? There is also compassion constantly taking place on an incredible scale, documented throughout history. There is always something else going on as well, if this were not so, the world would have been swallowed up by evils of one kind or another long ago, as it is, there is a silver lining in life, while not seen by all, has constantly shone in the darkness, 'and the darkness has not put it out'. (John 1) There is, as Philip Yancey puts it, rumours of another world.[120]

Both in nature and in humanity there is much beauty and much ugliness. There are both, an undeniable fact. And sometimes they run alongside each other – as recorded in this book, good, compassion, active in the midst of war for example, courage, self-sacrifice, and love in action in the midst of hate. And love present profoundly so in some of the worst circumstances in our world, in some of the worst disasters, a flowering of the human spirit, and incredible attitudes and acts of love.

'The other world' Philip Yancey writes about, points to that other world Jesus spoke about 'the kingdom of heaven'. This is radical, this is a kingdom built not on economic, military, political or monetary power but on love. By loving your neighbour as yourself, you value yourself, you value others, and you even value your enemy. For loving your enemy means you want the best for all concerned in a dispute, your enemy and yourself. And in so doing you actually show love for the author of this kind of love, a vulnerable God, for love is vulnerable, but which I have

120 'Rumours of Another World', Philip Yancey, Zondervan, 2003

tried to show in those pages is power, the paradox of love is the enigma of love.

"It has been said we should cling to the powerless, non-dominant Christ who has nothing more to persuade us with than his love. Christ's very powerlessness constitutes an inner personal authority; not because he begat, created, or made us, are we his, but simply because his only power is love, and this love, without any weapons, is stronger than death itself."

It is crucial for our world that the kind of love Jesus spoke of and lived is learnt and lived, developed and increased. The words of Jesus to love are recognised as the most realistic we can put into practice. When we live these words we are living in the kingdom of heaven Jesus spoke of. We are fulfilling the words of the Lord's Prayer 'thy kingdom come on earth as it is in heaven'; this is living the spiritual life.

Rowan Williams, Archbishop of Canterbury, has said, "Spirituality is the cultivation of a sensitive and rewarding relationship with eternal truth and love."

Steve Chalked on the first Christmas after the atrocities of September 11th interviewed a well-known American minister and theologian for a network breakfast television show in the U.K. ... here is the account of that interview ...

"Since it was Christmas Day I invited him to come into the studio to talk about the Christian message and how we can apply it to our world. I opened by asking him what Christmas was about for him....he replied, Jesus is the Prince of Peace...

'So if Jesus is the Prince of Peace and one of his key messages was love your enemies, what does that mean on a world scale?' I asked. 'How should it affect American foreign policy? What is your message to world leaders this Christmas?' 'I think it's easier to understand Jesus' message on a person-to-person level. It doesn't necessarily apply to nation/state relationships,' was his short reply.

We have been deluded into believing a myth that is destroying us. As Bono sings in U2's song 'Peace on Earth', 'Who said that if you go in hard you won't get hurt?' The ultimate weakness of violence, however, is that whenever it is employed, at whatever level – personal, community, national or global – it is a descending spiral. It begets the very thing it seeks to destroy.

… Even today, despite the claim that many of Western civilization's roots are to be found in the Christian faith and an almost universal admiration and respect for leaders such as Gandhi, Martin Luther King and Nelson Mandela, the myth still thrives that violence is the only solution to many of the world's problems. As the American author Jim Wallis has pointed out, Jesus' words 'Love your enemies' probably amount to the most admired but least practised piece of teaching in history. More often than not, Jesus' advice about non-violence is viewed as impractical idealism. Extraordinarily, though, no such charge is ever made against violence, in spite of history proving time and again that war and hostility solves nothing in the long run.

Despite thousands of years of individual, tribal and international bloodshed, the last century managed to produce the most horrific wars ever seen ...."[121]

---

121 'The Lost Message of Jesus, Zondervan, 2003 pp.127,129

Paul, a devout religious Jew, was eaten up with hatred for the followers of Jesus, a fellow Jew. He had a kind of fanatical religious hatred that leads to violence (in the Bible – Acts 9:1-2). He met Jesus, and therefore was able to write 1 Corinthians 13, that most famous passage on love, and as we have noted, he even puts love above faith. Even though he was the great expounder of faith in the New Testament (i.e. his letter to the Romans on justification by faith) he regarded love as more important. Jesus held love as of supreme importance, and on meeting Jesus, Paul realised that there was something far more important than even doctrines, for doctrines and traditions without love are nothing.

It is love that can bind us all together, Jew and Gentile; it will bridge all religious, political and cultural barriers. There is this absolute in life which brings people together in understanding and peace.

It is this that would solve the problems of conflict today. How wonderful it would be for example if Israelis and Palestinians were concerned first and foremost for each other's welfare, to consider the others needs before one's own. And in other areas of conflict, if the needs of those in conflict with more wealthy nations would be addressed instead of fighting, giving, to raise the standards of living. Poverty can often be a cause for anger by the poorer, resentment leading to aggression. The principle should be that which is spelt out in Luke 6:27 "Love your enemies, do good to those who hate you, bless those who curse you, pray for those who ill treat you."

Gandhi never renounced his Hindu faith, but believed in the same absolute as Martin Luther King, a Baptist minister, and Thich Nhat Hanh, a Buddhist monk. Jesus in his group of disciples included a Zealot (a kind of guerrilla fighter of the time), and a man that worked for Rome as a tax collector. He brought them together to work together in love, and for love.

It is sad that some Christian writers and preachers do not acknowledge that the absolute is not conforming to a particular creedal statement pattern or tradition or holding on to a particular doctrine, but to the absolute of compassionate love which is so crucial for us and our world.

The good news I have sought to share in this work is to declare that the values of the kingdom of Heaven are to be seen in this world. In spite of all the darkness there is the light of a hope that is everlasting. There are daily miracles of love expressed in homes, in communities, in the world, there is a silver lining in life, and we are encouraged to follow this way. This is the good news we bring to the world, that salvation is love that overcomes hate. At the height of his ministry Jesus' victory on that cross was the power of love over hate; and the eternal power of love, declares itself as indestructible in resurrection.

Cannon Vanstone states "the story of Jesus and especially his death and resurrection assures us that there is no greater power in the universe than emphatic love ... faith in love's triumph is neither more nor less than faith in the creator himself. Faith that he will not cease from his handiwork nor abandon the object of his love."[122]

Thus we see the creator. Love is manifest in the creator's

---

122 'Love's Endeavour, Love's Expense'

remembrance of us. Because of this love we are never lost to him. And not only does this love have the power to regenerate, not only the power to provide a new kind of body for that which is essentially me, but also is concerned with the renewal of the 'moral' person. Love woos and because this love is eternal there are no boundaries to its patience in this process.

We read in Colossians the whole of nature is renewed with the renewal of humanity, a nature therefore no longer red in tooth and claw, but one where the lion lies down with the lamb (Colossians 1:15-20' Isaiah 11:6-9; Romans 8:18-25). Thus it is seen at last that this love, that does not use violence or brute force to achieve its ends, brings a unity and beauty about, in the recreation of the whole cosmos.

There are those that diminish the victory of love, who accept a doctrine that still allows bitterness and regret to continue in an eternal torture chamber of some sort. When propounding views of eternal destiny that include hell, never it appears to me, do they have much to say about the problem of suffering in relation to hell, where it continues for ever – this is not good news and it devalues the greatest value of all, and to hold such a view has missed the importance of love, as ultimate victory.

The love which we have been researching is supremely good news. The universe including humanity does have a happy ending. It is encouraging to know that there are those who are eager to discover more about the kind of love we have been investigating. "A recent news item drew attention to the creation of a new institute for research on unlimited love in the medical school of the University of Ohio, partly inspired by Sorokin's work, and devoted 'to progress in the scientific understanding and practise of such remarkable phenomena as altruism, compassion and service."[123]

Because of this love there is hope for the present and hope for the future. I have sought to root the evidence for this in concrete situations in our world, and in endeavouring to grapple with the problem of the love of God and suffering. I have understood the author of life as vulnerable, bringing life out of vulnerability. Writing from within the Christian tradition, I see this love embodied in Jesus of Nazareth, as the one who lived this love in life here, and who therefore was concerned to give hope and healing in the present, but who also declared this message of love to have an eternal dimension to it. Out of the vulnerable came life for the present that would be fully revealed in a future glory, Jesus' resurrection proclaimed salvation out of fragmentation, the brokenness of the cross results in the glory of resurrection. The pattern for humanity, a new body for a new sphere, a continuity and discontinuity.

As John Polkinghorne puts it, "There must be sufficient continuity to ensure that individuals truly share in the life to come as their resurrected selves and not as new beings simply given old names. There must be sufficient discontinuity to ensure that the life to come is free from suffering and mortality of the old creation."[124]

And so I have seen this love as overflowing on into eternity as in 'Beyond the Horizon', 'Love and Human Destiny'. But

---

123 Quoted in 'Comparative Theology; essays for Keith Ward', SPCK, 2003 p.185

124 'The God of Hope and the End of the World, SPCK, 2002 p.149

whether dealing with aspects of love in life situations, or with aspects of life after death, or with the person of God, that which is the source of love, and the central place of love embodied in Jesus of Nazareth, I have endeavoured always to root all in real life situations pointing to that which we call eternal life. All this being possible because love as a fact is our hope, our positive hope, and is operating for good in the present, representative of that other kingdom, the kingdom of Heaven.

The love written about here comes from the very spirit of life which in Christian terms one can see as the Holy Spirit at work. Jurgen Moltmann has written,

"… because in this experience of life we come close to the eternal origin of all things, those powers of life are also powers of the future world. They are powers which come into our mortal life here from the eternal life on the other side of death, and kindle the beginning of the life which reaches beyond death.

The faithfulness of God in history, Christ's resurrection, and the experience of life in God's Spirit are the grounds for the expectation of eternal life in God's future new world. We are only drawing the conclusions, and tracing the horizons of the hope which springs from these foundations. And in so doing we arrive at eternal life."[125]

So this love moves through this world in this one and that. It operates because the life of the Spirit, the love that creates, brings hope and evidence of this love's reality. It is paradoxical, it is weak yet strong, vulnerable yet eternal.

---

125 'In the End, the Beginning', SCM, 2003 p.164

Paul Fiddes echoing Cannon Vanstone writes "The risks of love are real, corresponding to the real gains of love. But the story of Jesus, and especially his death and resurrection, assures us that there is no greater power in the universe than emphatic love."[126]

---

126 From his essay in 'The Work of Love', Ed John Polkinghorne, SPCK, Eerdmans, 2001 pp.189-190

Bibliography

Blanchard John, Whatever happened to Hell, Evangelical Press 1993

Barclay William, Commentary on Matthew's Gospel, St Andrews Press 1975, and New Testament Words, SCM, 1964

Brown Malcolm and Seaton Shirley, CHRISTMAS TRUCE, Pan Books 2001

Chapman Colin, the Case for Christianity, Lion 1981

Craig Masy, Candles in the Dark, Hodder (Spire) 1984

Clements Roy, Practising Faith in a Pagan World, I.V.P. 1997

Clements. Roy, The Strength of Weakness, Christian Focus 1996

Chalke .Steve, The LOST MESSAGE of Jesus. Zondervan 2003

Clayton. David, Hell Fact or Fiction?, Athena Press 2006

Ellsberg. Robert, Thich Nhat Hanh, Essential Writings, Orbis 2001

Flew. Antony, There is a God, Harper One 2007

Fischer. Kathleen, Imaging Life after Death, SPCK 2005

Fiddes. Paul in, The Work of Love, Ed. John Polkinghorne, Creation out of Love, SPCK 2001

Graham. Billy, Living in God's Love

Holloway. Richard, Doubts and Loves, Canongate 2001

Hodges. David, Do we Survive Death, Pilgrim Trust 2004

His Holiness the Dali Lama, Widening the Circle of Love, Rider Publications 2002

Humphrys. John, In God we Doubt, Confessions of a Failed Atheist, Hodder 2007

Harries. Richard, God outside the Box, SPCK 2002

Hick. John, The Fifth Dimension, One World, 1999

Israel. Martin, Life Eternal, SPCK 1993

Jamison. Abbot Christopher, Finding Sanctuary

Jones. Martyn Lloyd, Authority, Banner of Truth Trust 1958

Kenneth. Brother, Saints of the 20th Century, Mowbrays 1976

Kuschel. Karl Josef, Tolstoy quoted in The Poet as a Mirror, SCM 1997

Kung. Hans, Eternal Life, Collins 1984

Lucas. Jeff, Spring Harvest Study Guide

Lennox. John, God's Undertaker, Lion 2007

Moltmann. Jurgen, Theology of Hope, SCM 1967, 2002

Macmillan. Encyclopaedia 1981

Mooney. Bell, Ed. Devout Sceptics, Hodder 2003

McGrath. Alister, The Dawkins Delusion, SPCK 2007

McGrath. Alister, Glimpsing the Face of God, Lion 2002

McGrath. Alister, Dawkins God, Blackwell Publisher 2005

O'Collins. Gerald, Easter Faith, DLT 2003

Polkinghorne. John, The God of Hope and the End of the World, SPCK 2002

Polkinghorne. John, Exploring Reality, SPCK 2005

Polkinghorne. John, and Beale, Questions of Truth (Faith)? WJK 2009

Polkinghorne. John, Belief in Age of Science, Yale 1998

Polkinghorne. John, Living with Hope, SPCK 2003

Popescu. D. Alexandru, Petre Tutea, Between Sacrifice and Suicide, Aldershot, Ashgate 2004

Radcliff. Timothy, Seven Last Words, Burns and Oats Continuum 2006

Radcliffe Timothy, What is the Point of being a Christian? Burns and Oates Continuum 2005

Ramsey. Michael, Sacred and Secular, Longmans 1965

Rahner. Karl, Experiences of a Catholic Theologian, 1984

Peacock. Arthur, In the Work of Love, SPCK 2001

Spong. John Shelby, Myth and Reality, Harper Collins

Strobel. Lee, The Case for Easter

Spoto. Donald, The Hidden Jesus, St Martins Press 1998

Sykes. William, Visions of Love, Bible Reading Fellowship 1992

Simmons. Learning to Fall, Hodder 2002

Vanstone. W.H., Love's Endeavour, Love's Expense, from the work of Love, ed John Polkinghorne. SPCK 2001

Wilson. Gordon, with Alf McCreary, Maria, Marshal and Pickering 1990

Woodhouse. Patrick, A Life Transformed, Etty Hillesum, Continuum 2009

Ward. Keith, What the Bible Really Says, SPCK 2004

Ward. Keith, Christianity, a Guide for the Perplexed, SPCK 2007

Ward. Keith, The Case for Religion, One World 2004

Ward. Keith, Comparative Theology Essays for Keith Ward

White. Vernon, Life Beyond Death, DLT 2006

Winston. Albert, The Story of God, Bantam Press

Yancy. Philip, Where is God when it hurts, Zondervan 1997

Yancy. Philip, Rumours of another World, Zondervan 2003